RAND

Financial Crises and Contagion in Emerging Market Countries

Julia Lowell, C. Richard Neu, Daochi Tong

National Security Research Division

PREFACE

This study explores why some financial crises appear to be contagious, and why some financial markets in emerging market countries appear to be vulnerable to contagion while others are not. To begin, multicountry crisis episodes for the period January 1989 to August 1997 are identified and analyzed using statistical methods. Next, four informal models of contagion are developed and sets of indicators proposed. Finally, case studies are used to illustrate the usefulness of the models and indicators for explaining the experience of three countries with potentially contagious financial crises.

This research was conducted within RAND's National Security Research Division (NSRD), which does work for the U.S. Department of Defense, for other U.S. government agencies, and for other sponsoring institutions.

CONTENTS

TABLES

SUMMARY

Why do some crises appear to be contagious, and why do some emerging financial markets appear to be vulnerable to contagion while others are not? Defining a crisis as a very large decline in either the U.S. dollar value of the local currency or a broad-based stock price index, this study proposes three reasons why countries might experience crises at the same, or close to the same, time: (1) coincidence, (2) a common external shock to economic conditions across countries, and (3) a contagious loss of confidence in local financial markets as a result of an external financial crisis. We argue that, to the extent that crises are coincidental--that is, country-specific in origin--in many if not most cases they should be both predictable and preventable with the help of traditional economic warning signals. To the extent that crises are externally generated, however, traditional warning signals may be of little use.

Using weekly stock and currency price data for January 1989 through August 1997, we identify and examine episodes in which very large swings in asset prices occurred simultaneously or nearly simultaneously across financial markets in four or more countries. Eleven such episodes are found, of which the majority appear to be explained by purely country-specific factors rather than a common shock or contagion. Given the evidence on the probability distributions of asset price movements, we conclude that this is not an unreasonable observation.

A formal statistical analysis of four of the episodes--the August 1990 Gulf War crisis, a rash of crises spanning January-June 1994, the December 1994-March 1995 Mexican peso crisis, and the July-August 1997 Thai baht crisis--reveals that, in the first two episodes, there is little evidence that U.S. stock price movements were responsible for stock market collapses in the countries involved. This finding is consistent with the hypothesis that these two episodes were *not* triggered by financial market events in the United States. During the 24 months surrounding the respective devaluations of the Mexican peso and Thai baht, however, we reject the hypothesis that multicountry stock and currency market collapses were generally independent of events in Mexican and Thai currency markets.

To explore the implication of contagion for the predictability and preventability of crises in individual countries, four informal models of the transmission mechanisms that may operate during a contagious crisis episode are developed. The first model, the "economic linkages" model, describes the case in which a foreign financial crisis acts as a common shock to countries with strong economic linkages to the country in crisis. The second model, "heightened awareness," suggests that investors with incomplete information may ignore poor economic conditions in some countries until a crisis occurs somewhere else, at which point they dump their investments in those countries. The "portfolio adjustment" model describes what happens when liquidity--constrained portfolio managers sell off other countries' assets in order to meet an expected increase in redemptions from a country in crisis. The "herd behavior" model is probably the most widely accepted view of contagion, suggesting that investors abandon their investments largely in response to what they think other investors are doing.

The four contagion models have different implications for the predictability and preventability of multicountry crises. Contagious crisis episodes caused by economic linkages between countries are most likely predictable once the first crisis occurs, but there may be little that downstream countries can do to prevent them. Crises caused by investors with incomplete information might be avoided by better reporting and analysis of relevant data and, of course, by better macroeconomic policies. Portfolio-adjustment type crises are fairly predictable as long as, in the aggregate, portfolio composition remains the same over time and across managers. Finally, the only defense against crises caused by herd behavior may be the introduction of capital controls, which themselves entail significant costs.

A brief review of the theoretical and empirical literature leads us to conclude that traditional indicators of financial crises often do not perform well in the context of externally generated financial shocks. Using these four models, therefore, we propose a set of contagion-vulnerability indicators. We conclude with an informal examination of the usefulness of our contagion indicators in the context of three recent crisis experiences: Argentina after the devaluation of the Mexican peso in December 1994, South Africa's currency crisis of 1996, and Southeast Asia after the devaluation of the Thai baht in July 1997. The case studies suggest that the contagion indicators we propose are a promising avenue for future research on emerging market countries' vulnerability to financial contagion.

ACKNOWLEDGMENTS

The authors would like to thank, without implicating, Douglas Steigerwald, Menzie Chinn, Helen Popper, and William Maloney for their helpful comments and criticisms. We would also like to thank participants in RAND's *Roundtable on International Financial Contagion* (Washington, D.C., June 1997), as well as participants in seminars at Santa Cruz and Langley, VA, and at the conference *Charting East Asia's Economic Prospects: Should We Still Believe in Miracles?* (Arlington, VA, November 5-6, 1997). Useful suggestions were also made during interviews with economists at Chase Manhattan's Global Emerging Markets Division, J.P. Morgan's Fixed Income & Emerging Markets Research Group, and the Federal Reserve Bank of New York.

1. INTRODUCTION

In the wake of recent balance-of-payments crises in Mexico (1994-1995) and Thailand (1997) and their spillovers to other emerging market countries (EMCs), there has been renewed interest in the origins of multicountry financial crises and the nature of their cross-border transmission. U.S. analysts and policymakers in particular would like to know why some crises appear to be contagious, and why some EMC financial markets appear to be vulnerable to contagion while others do not.

U.S. concern about international financial contagion is justified on economic grounds for at least three reasons. First, widespread financial market failures on the scale of the Mexican and Thai collapses threaten to derail EMC policies aimed at deregulating domestic markets and opening them to foreign competition. Second, U.S. policymakers would like to minimize the likelihood that the role of international lender-of-last-resort will fall to the United States. Third, some of the United States' most important trade and investment partners are emerging market countries. Financial market turbulence in EMCs therefore directly affects U.S. economic interests.

Unfortunately, neither the causes of multicountry financial crises nor the mechanisms by which they are transmitted across borders are well understood. In recent episodes of apparent contagion, some EMC officials have blamed capricious foreign speculators for sparking massive capital outflows, currency market turbulence, and the collapse of local stock markets in countries downstream from the original source of collapse.[1] They argue that investors simply followed the lead of speculators, abandoning sound investments on the flimsiest of economic rationales. This view of financial contagion suggests that it is analogous to a medical epidemic: destructive, unpredictable, and largely unrelated to macroeconomic developments in downstream countries.

---

[1] Consider, for example, President Mahathir of Malaysia's well-publicized remarks that his country's ongoing financial crisis has been manipulated by foreign speculators (*The Economist*, 1997a).

A sharply contrasting view is that all financial crises, including what look like contagious crises, are simply rational investor responses to local economic misfortune or, more probably, to economic mismanagement by local governments. In this view, country-specific political and economic developments explain both when and why countries experience crises; speculators are simply the first to realize the significance of these developments. Thus, financial difficulties in one country should have little effect on financial markets in another country unless there are strong economic linkages between the two.

Why should it matter which view of financial contagion is closest to the truth? One reason is that fear of contagion makes developing countries wary of exposing their infant capital markets to sudden and irrational investor behavior over which they have no control. In response, they may place restrictions on cross-border capital flows, thereby reducing the efficiency of the international financial system.[2] Another reason is that, if the second view of contagion is correct, the right set of economic indicators ought to make crises predictable--and perhaps preventable. If crises *aren't* random, "getting the fundamentals right" becomes both a necessary and sufficient strategy for avoiding them altogether.

In this study, we define a financial crisis as a sudden decline in investor demand for a financial asset that plays an important role in the domestic economy. The resulting fall in the asset price reduces aggregate economic activity directly through its impact on the decisions of individual consumers and firms, and indirectly through its effects on the prices of other assets and on the balance sheets of financial intermediaries such as banks.[3] We consider two types of potentially contagious crises:

- stock market crashes

---

[2] For example, Chile, Colombia, and Brazil have imposed taxes on inflows and outflows of short-term capital; Indonesia, Malaysia, Mexico, the Philippines, and Thailand have imposed quantity restrictions on certain types of capital inflows (IMF, 1995).

[3] Mishkin (1991) provides a thoughtful discussion of the types of events that should be considered "crises."

- currency (balance of payments) crises.[4]

Both are representative of recent international experience, can have severe economic consequences, and are the focus of current international efforts to prevent future contagious episodes.

Explaining Contemporaneous Crises

There are at least three reasons why different countries might experience severe downward pressure on prices of financial assets at the same, or close to the same, time. The first is simple coincidence: each country's experience is driven by purely idiosyncratic factors. For example, an economic development unfavorable to investments in one country might take place at the same time as similar types of events elsewhere. In this case there is no sense in which one country's financial difficulties contribute to the difficulties experienced by the others; each country brings its troubles on itself. In many cases these crises are caused by bad policy, and should be both predictable and preventable.

The second reason concerns asset price movements that are related to each other by a common external shock. A relevant historical example here is the jump in the world price of oil that occurred at the onset of the Gulf War in August 1990. A less dramatic example, but one quite relevant to developing capital markets, might be a rise in U.S. interest rates. In both examples, external economic or political developments alter the fundamental economic conditions that underlie investor valuations of local financial assets. Unfortunately, local policymakers have little power to prevent this sort of crisis, and traditional crisis warning signals have almost as little power to predict it.

The third explanation for a multicountry financial crisis is contagion, that is, a loss of confidence in local financial assets that

---

[4] Currency crises may or may not also be accompanied by a crash of the local stock market and the widespread insolvency of local financial institutions. But all currency crises involve net outflows of capital as investors sell off their local-currency-denominated assets in an attempt to reap gains or prevent losses from the actual or expected decline in the value of the currency.

is caused by a financial crisis in another country. The key distinction here is that investors downgrade their estimations of the risk/return trade-offs for a country's financial assets despite unchanged local economic fundamentals. A crash somewhere else is sufficient to send asset markets spiraling downward, with the set of countries affected depending on noneconomic factors such as geographic proximity or linguistic and cultural ties. As in the case of a common shock, traditional crisis warning signals are likely to be ineffective because the crisis is externally generated. The policy tools available to prevent contagious crises are also likely to be blunt.

Many multicountry crises probably contain elements of all three explanations. For example, the factors that contributed to the spread of Thailand's financial difficulties to other countries in the region in 1997 probably included weak but not demonstrably deteriorating local banking systems, a common external shock (the devaluation of the baht) that reduced export competitiveness, and uninformed but widespread investor concern about the financial health of the region overall. Although there were few traditional warning signals of an impending regional crisis, the fallout from the collapse of the baht was, nevertheless, predictable. These points are argued at greater length below.

Plan of the Paper

In Chapter 2 of this study, we examine episodes in which very large drops in asset prices occurred simultaneously or nearly simultaneously across financial markets in several countries. For the period spanning January 1989 to August 1997, we identify eleven episodes that involved multiple EMC markets. English-language press accounts and official reports by multinational institutions are used as the basis for classifying each episode according to the triggering event, which may be a "common external shock," "country-specific shock," or "contagion." We conclude that the majority of episodes we identify were probably country-specific in origin, and that this is not inconsistent with informal calculations of probability.

In Chapter 3, we analyze more formally four of the eleven multicountry crisis episodes identified in Chapter 2. The episodes we examine are the August 1990 Gulf War crisis, a rash of crises spanning January-June 1994, the December 1994-March 1995 Mexican peso crisis, and the July-August 1997 Thai baht crisis.[5] Using regional as well as single-country causality tests, we attempt to distinguish between contagion type and common-shock or country-specific type crisis episodes using statistical methods. In general, our results support the popular wisdom that contagion was a greater factor in the Mexican and Thai crises than in the first two crisis episodes.

In Chapter 4, we briefly review the available evidence on the determination and prediction of stock and currency market crises. We then introduce four informal models of financial contagion and discuss their implications for both the predictability and preventability of contagious crises. On the basis of these models, we propose a set of variables that may act as indicators as well as determinants of the vulnerability of downstream countries to contagious crises.

Finally, in Chapter 5 we present three case studies of countries that represent different types of financial crises and different experiences with contagion. The first case, Argentina during the Mexican crisis of 1994-1995, is a classic contagion story involving both stock and currency market crises. The second case, which describes South Africa's financial difficulties in 1996, stands in contrast to the Mexican crisis because it generated no contagion. The third and last case assesses the performance of the contagion-vulnerability indicators in the context of the ongoing economic and financial crisis in East Asia. In Chapter 6 we formulate our conclusions based on this research.

---

[5] The crisis sparked by the devaluation of the Thai baht is of course still unfolding, but our data sample ends in August 1997.

2. CRISIS IDENTIFICATION

The Data

Our sample consists of 17 EMCs chosen for their political and economic importance to the United States, the level of their financial market development, and the availability of relevant data. It also includes six financial markets chosen for their importance as either world or regional financial centers. Table 2.1 lists the countries in the sample.

Table 2.1

Country Sample

Emerging Market Countries			
Argentina	Hungary	Mexico	Taiwan
Brazil	India	Philippines	Thailand
Chile	Indonesia	Poland	Turkey
China	Malaysia	South Africa	Venezuela
Czech Republic			
Financial Centers			
Germany (Frankfurt)	Japan (Tokyo)	United Kingdom (London)	
Hong Kong	Singapore	United States (New York)	

The data consist of national stock price indices, currency exchange rates, and foreign exchange reserves for each country in the sample. For the EMCs, weekly local currency data, EMC stock price index data, and currency exchange rate data for January 1989 through August 1997 were obtained from the International Finance Corporation's (IFC) Emerging Markets Database, a database widely used by investment analysts and portfolio managers.[6] Over the same sample period, weekly stock price and exchange rate data for the six financial centers were obtained

[6] Although monthly data from the IFC's Emerging Markets Database are available from 1987 for some countries, weekly data are available only from January 1989.

from Datastream International. Monthly data on foreign reserves less gold were obtained from the International Monetary Fund series *International Financial Statistics.*[7]

The IFC stock price indices are constructed from Friday closing prices for a large sample of stocks in each market. We examine the local-currency-denominated indices, as opposed to U.S.-dollar-denominated indices, in order not to confuse shifts in stock market demand with exchange rate movements. More information on the construction of the indices is available from the International Finance Corporation (1996). The IFC currency exchange rates are based on the Friday closing prices of local currency in terms of the U.S. dollar.[8]

Identification of Crises

We begin by log differencing the stock and currency market variables so that they follow the form $x_{it} = \ln(X_{it}/X_{it-1}) * 100$, where X represents the variable in levels, i is the market index, and t represents the weekly or monthly time index. For each financial market variable in each country, we define a financial collapse to be a movement in x_{it} that is more than two standard deviations below the mean.[9] While this is consistent with our overall interpretation of a financial crisis, the choice of two standard deviations is arbitrary; a normally distributed x_{it} would imply that approximately 2.5 percent of the observations would be defined as collapses.

---

[7] Examination of foreign exchange reserves is necessary in order to capture possible currency market crises that did *not* result in changes to a pegged regime. However, because the reserves data are available only monthly, crises associated with large movements in foreign reserves are attributed to an entire month rather than a particular week. Unfortunately, appropriate time series data on interest rates, which would also help to capture exchange rate pressure, are not easily available for many of the countries in the sample.

[8] In certain cases, the IFC has substituted black market or other rates of exchange for official U.S. dollar exchange rates in an effort to reflect the true U.S. dollar price of local currency stocks. In the two instances of IFC substitution that we identified, our analysis was not affected.

[9] Exchange rates are measured in terms of U.S. dollars, except for the U.S. dollar, which is measured in terms of an IMF Special Drawing Rights (SDR) basket. For exchange rates, collapses are two standard deviations above the mean.

Two aspects of our identification methodology are worth noting. First, the methodology implies that a collapse for one country may be a mere ripple for another. We believe that this is appropriate because crises are experienced differentially. For example, in Argentina, a 3 percent drop in the stock market is not unusual, and so is viewed with some complacency. In the United States or South Africa, however, a 3 percent stock market decline is highly unusual and cause for considerable concern. The second noteworthy aspect of our methodology is the rather mechanical way of defining a financial crisis as an asset price collapse of a certain magnitude. Ideally, we would like to capture all rapid and unexpected asset price movements that have the potential to destabilize an economy. Unfortunately, such a definition is impossible to operationalize in practice. Our method may miss some legitimate crises, or wrongly include some merely robust financial readjustments, but it should not matter too much: The focus of this paper is on the communication of disturbances, not on crises *per se*.

In Table 2.2, collapses in stock prices, currency values, and foreign reserves are characterized for each country in the sample. For each variable in each country, the first column of the table presents the "collapse boundary," or the percentage decline beyond which we consider a collapse to have occurred. The second column presents the number of observations falling below the boundary, and the third column presents the share of the sample represented by collapses. From column 1, for example, we see that the average stock price collapse boundary for the EMCs in the sample was 9.2 percent, which compares to 4.3 percent for the financial centers as a whole, and 2.9 percent for the United States. On average, the countries in the sample experienced stock price collapses 5.1 percent of the time, currency collapses 2.6 percent of the time, and sharp drops in foreign reserves 6.5 percent of the time. This suggests that, consistent with findings in the empirical literature, the x_{it} are not distributed as normal random variables.[10]

[10] Candidate distributions for modeling both exchange rates and stock prices include the *t* and exponential power distributions. See, for example, Baillie and Bollerslev (1989) and Nelson (1991).

Table 2.2

Large Asset Price and Reserves Collapses
January 1989 to August 1997

Emerging Market/ Financial Center	Stock Price Index: Collapse Boundary (percent)	Stock Price Index: Number of Collapses	Stock Price Index: Collapses as Percent of Sample	Currency Value[a]: Collapse Boundary (percent)	Currency Value[a]: Number of Collapses	Currency Value[a]: Collapses as Percent of Sample	Foreign Reserves: Collapse Boundary (percent)	Foreign Reserves: Number of Collapses	Foreign Reserves: Collapses as Percent of Sample
Asia									
China[b]	14.6	5	2.5	4.1	7	3.5	13.3	2	2.1
India	7.6	21	4.7	2.2	15	3.3	24.4	5	4.9
Indonesia[c]	6.3	18	5.0	1.7	8	2.2	9.5	8	7.8
Malaysia	5.5	24	5.3	1.2	14	3.1	11.2	7	7.2
Philippines	7.1	24	5.3	2.6	14	3.1	28.2	7	6.9
Taiwan	9.8	26	5.8	1.3	20	4.4	na	na	na
Thailand	8.6	21	4.7	1.9	10	2.2	4.2	3	2.9
Latin America									
Argentina	17.6	22	4.9	15.9	16	3.5	29.1	9	8.7
Brazil	12.2	18	4.0	11.2	14	3.1	15.5	10	9.8
Chile	5.1	25	5.5	2.1	20	4.4	5.5	5	4.9
Mexico	5.5	18	4.0	4.4	16	3.5	32.1	8	7.8
Venezuela	9.0	20	4.4	8.4	6	1.3	13.2	8	7.8
Europe									
Czech Rep.[d]	7.4	11	7.5	1.8	4	2.7	na	na	na
Hungary[b]	6.9	11	5.6	2.5	9	4.5	18.9	5	5.4
Poland[b]	15.0	12	6.1	2.2	8	4.0	9.9	6	5.9
Turkey	13.7	25	5.5	5.9	9	2.0	17.3	6	5.8

Table 2.2- continued

Emerging Market/ Financial Center	Stock Price Index			Currency Value[a]			Foreign Reserves		
	Collapse Boundary (percent)	Number of Collapses	Collapses as Percent of Sample	Collapse Boundary (percent)	Number of Collapses	Collapses as Percent of Sample	Collapse Boundary (percent)	Number of Collapses	Collapses as Percent of Sample
Africa									
South Africa[b]	4.0	13	6.6	3.9	11	5.6	37.1	6	5.9
EMC AVERAGE	9.2	18.5	5.1	4.3	11.8	3.3	18.0	6.3	6.3
Financial Centers									
Germany	3.8	23	5.1	3.0	7	1.6	16.0	4	3.9
Hong Kong	6.0	24	5.3	0.2	0	0.0	na	na	na
Japan	5.4	24	5.3	2.9	0	0.0	5.1	11	10.7
Singapore	4.3	19	4.2	0.9	0	0.0	1.5	6	5.9
United Kingdom	3.3	21	4.7	2.9	8	1.8	6.5	8	7.9
United States	2.9	22	4.9	1.5	0	0.0	6.9	8	7.8
CENTER AVERAGE	4.3	22.2	4.9	1.9	2.5	0.6	7.2	7.4	7.2
SAMPLE AVERAGE	7.9	23	5.1	3.7	12	2.6	15.3	7	6.5

[a]Currency exchange rates against U.S. dollar except for U.S. dollar, which is measured against a Special Drawing Rights (SDR) currency basket.

[b]Data begin 1/1/93 and end 10/18/96.

[c]Data begin 10/05/90.

[d]Data begin 1/07/94 and end 10/18/96.

Several interesting patterns emerge from this procedure. Across asset markets, sharp declines in stock market values occur more frequently than declines in currency values. This reflects the fact that even those countries with nominally floating-rate exchange regimes generally employ at least some degree of exchange rate management.[11] But as we might expect, exchange rate movements alone turn out to be a poor measure of currency market pressure: For the majority of countries, large declines in official foreign exchange reserves over the period occurred even more frequently than drops in the stock market.

Cross-country patterns also emerge from the data. Large movements in exchange rates appear much less often in the financial centers than in EMCs. In fact, only two of the six financial centers included in our sample--Germany and the United Kingdom--experienced any exchange rate movements that were outside their two standard deviation bands. Reserve movements in the more financially developed countries were also well below the average for the sample. Stock markets also appear to be more stable in the financial centers. The largest stock market, New York, is the least volatile, closely followed by London and Frankfurt. The country with the most volatile stock market, Argentina, also has the dubious distinction of having the most volatile exchange rate and, second only to Mexico, the most volatile foreign reserves.

Identification of Possibly Contagious Crises

Our main interest, however, is not to characterize asset price collapses in individual countries, but rather to identify and examine possible episodes of cross-border financial contagion. For each possibly contagious episode, we would like to identify the countries and markets that were involved, as well as the duration of the episode.

Our strategy involves two stages of data analysis. First, we identify individual weeks in which there were overlapping outside-the-band movements in currency or equity markets that involved four or more countries. This procedure captures strictly contemporaneous asset price collapses. Next, to establish duration, we extend the episode on both

---

[11] Popper and Lowell (1994) provide evidence on this point.

sides of the four-plus crisis overlap until we reach a four-week buffer period in which two or fewer crisis overlaps occurred. The episodes we identify thus vary in duration from one week to six months.[12] The choice of number of overlaps and buffer period length is arbitrary, designed to capture the best-known crisis episodes while minimizing the total number of crises identified. For the period 1989 to 1997, this procedure identifies a total of thirteen financial crisis episodes. Upon closer examination, we reduce the total to eleven.[13]

A brief description of the eleven crisis episodes, including the relevant time period and countries involved, is presented in Table 2.3. Columns 1 through 4 of the table indicate, respectively, the months and year of the crisis episode, the specific dates, the markets that were affected, and the countries that were involved. Column 5 identifies the week in which the maximum number of countries experienced collapses, while column 6 presents possible triggering events or contributing factors derived from the English-language financial press as well as publications of multinational financial institutions.[14]

Of the eleven episodes we identify, not one consists entirely of either stock- or currency-market collapses. However, consistent with the greater number of stock market collapses overall, seven of the eleven episodes primarily reflect stock market turbulence. This is especially true for episode 3, which took place in the two weeks

---

[12] There were three sets of episodes for which this duration constraint was binding or close to binding. In 1989, an episode in March and April was separated by only four weeks from an episode that began in June. In 1990, five weeks separated an August-September episode from an episode in November and December. In 1995, there were distinct January and March phases to what most consider to be a single crisis triggered by the collapse of the Mexican peso.

[13] A May 1995 episode involving currency markets in the Czech Republic, Hungary, Poland, and Germany was not a true multicountry episode because at the time the three EMC currencies were effectively tied to the German mark. (The mark depreciated sharply against the U.S. dollar on May 11 and 12 for reasons of its own.) The January and March 1995 phases of the Mexican peso crisis have been combined into one.

[14] Newspaper sources include *The New York Times, The Wall Street Journal, The Financial Times, The Asian Wall Street Journal,* and the *Los Angeles Times.* Magazine sources include *The Economist,* the *Far Eastern Economic Review, Euromoney,* and *Business Week.* Official sources include selected publications by the International Monetary Fund, World Bank, Asia Development Bank, Inter-American Development Bank, and Bank for International Settlements.

following the October 1989 U.S. stock market crash, and episode 5, which followed the onset of the Gulf War. Only episodes 1 and 7 were primarily currency market phenomena, and these do not appear to have been driven by a common event.

Causes and Characteristics of Crisis Episodes

Our first task is to categorize the episodes by their primary explanatory factors. On the basis of the public record evidence, the episodes are categorized as described in Table 2.4.

Episodes 2 and 5, the two common-shock episodes, are rather easy to identify: In both cases observers agree that external events (Tiananmen Square, onset of the Gulf War) were responsible for crashing stock markets in most of the countries that experienced crises. For Germany in episode 8, and several of the countries involved in episodes 4 and 9, English-language reports suggest that their troubles can be largely attributed to identifiable country-specific factors, such as political scandals or economic policies perceived to be unfavorable to investors. We found no English-language sources, however, that assign blame for episodes 1, 2 (non-Asian countries), 6, 7, or 8 (China, Mexico, Hong Kong). We posit that the collapses in these countries during these episodes were due to country-specific factors, and were of insufficient consequence to report to an international audience. Finally, financial contagion from abroad is blamed for the financial turbulence that affected most of the countries involved in episodes 3, 10, and 11; country-specific factors also appear to have been important for some of these countries.

An important and sensible question to ask is whether it is reasonable to attribute so many multicountry crisis episodes to country-specific events by default. As we noted in the Introduction, during such episodes, governments sometimes blame their own economic and financial troubles on external events over which they have no control. Are their arguments valid? What is the probability of four or more countries experiencing simultaneous yet unrelated financial collapses?

Table 2.3

Identification of Contagious Crisis Periods

Crisis Episode (Month/Year)	Crisis Dates	Market Affected	Countries Experiencing Crises	Max Overlap Week (Number of Countries)	Triggering Event / Contributing Factors
1. March-April 1989	3/24/89 to 4/28/89	Currency	Argentina, Chile, Mexico, Philippines	4/28/89 (4)	Unidentified country-specific events
		Stock	Turkey		
2. June 1989	6/02/89 to 6/30/89	Currency	Argentina, China, Indonesia, Japan	6/09/89 (8)	Asia: Tiananmen Square massacre on 6/4/89
		Stock	Brazil, Chile, Malaysia, Hong Kong, Singapore		Others: Unidentified country-specific events
3. October 1989	10/20/89 to 10/27/89	Currency	United Kingdom	10/20/89 (5)	U.S. stock market falls almost 7 percent on 10/13/89
		Stock	Malaysia, Turkey, Germany, Singapore, U.K., U.S.		
4. February-April 1990	2/23/90 to 4/06/90	Currency	Argentina, Brazil, Indonesia, Malaysia, Mexico, Taiwan, Japan, Singapore	3/23/90 (6)	Argentina, Brazil, Taiwan, Germany, Japan: Country-specific events[a]
		Stock	Brazil, Taiwan, Turkey, Germany, Japan, U.K.		Others unidentified
5. August-September 1990	8/10/90 to 9/28/90	Currency	Chile, Philippines	8/24/90 (12)	Gulf War: Iraq invades Kuwait on 8/2/90
		Stock	Malaysia, Mexico, Philippines, Taiwan, Thailand, Turkey, Germany, Hong Kong, Japan, Singapore, U.K., U.S.		

Table 2.3 - continued (1)

Crisis Episode (Month/Year)	Crisis Dates	Market Affected	Countries Experiencing Crises	Max Overlap Week (Number of Countries)	Triggering Event / Contributing Factors
6. November-December 1990	11/02/90 to 12/28/90	Currency	Brazil, Hungary, India, Poland	12/21/90 (6)	Hungary, Thailand: Country-specific events[b]
		Stock	India, Thailand, Turkey, Germany		Others unidentified
7. March 1991	3/01/91 to 3/29/91	Currency	Argentina, Brazil, Turkey, Japan, Singapore, U.S.	3/22/91 (6)	Argentina, Brazil: Country-specific events[c]
		Stock	Indonesia		Others unidentified
8. July 1992	7/24/92	Currency	China	7/24/92 (4)	Country-specific events[d]
		Stock	Mexico, Germany, Hong Kong		
9. January-June 1994	1/14/94 to 6/24/94	Currency	Mexico, South Africa, Turkey, Venezuela	3/04/94 (6)	Sharply rising U.S. interest rates throughout period
		Stock	Chile, Hungary, India, Indonesia, Malaysia, Philippines, Poland, South Africa, Turkey, Venezuela, Germany, Hong Kong, Singapore, U.K., U.S.		Some identifiable country-specific events[e]
10. January-March 1995	1/13/95 to 3/17/95	Currency	Argentina, Hungary, Malaysia, Mexico	1/13/95 (9)	Mexican peso devalued 15 percent on 12/20/94; allowed to float on 12/22/94; affects all EMCs.
		Stock	Brazil, Chile, China, Czech Republic, Hungary, Malaysia, Mexico, Philippines, Poland, South Africa, Turkey, Venezuela, Germany		Germany: Country-specific events

Table 2.3 - continued (2)

Crisis Episode (Month/Year)	Crisis Dates	Market Affected	Countries Experiencing Crises	Max Overlap Week (Number of Countries)	Triggering Event / Contributing Factors
11. July-August 1997	7/04/97 to 8/22/97 (end of sample)	Currency	Indonesia, Malaysia, Philippines, Thailand, Singapore	8/15/97 (7)	Bank of Thailand floats the baht; baht depreciates by more than 11 percent in week ending 7/4/97.
		Stock	Brazil, Indonesia, Malaysia, Philippines, Thailand, Germany, U.S.		

NOTE: [a]Argentina: Hyperinflation follows December 1989 devaluation.
Brazil: Cruzeiro replaces New Cruzado on March 13 at 1:1 conversion rate; Collor government introduces stock market turnover tax.
Taiwan: Uncertainty over presidential election spooks stock market and currency follows.
Germany: High interest rates and worries about effects of reunification.
Japan: Bank of Japan raises interest rates; yen follows stock market down.
[b]Hungary: Large reserve losses anticipating removal of capital controls and price increases.
Thailand: Weakening economy due to large oil price rises; political squabbling.
[c]Argentina: Austral devalued with dollarization plan begun March 20.
Brazil: Ongoing struggle with hyperinflation.
[d]China, Hong Kong: Concerns over Most-Favored-Nation trade status for China in U.S.
Mexico: Concern over economic growth and U.S. Presidential candidacy of Ross Perot.
Germany, Hong Kong: Sharp rise in German discount rate; record lows for U.S. dollar.
[e]Chile: Regulatory ruling against largest listed firm on stock exchange causes stock market plunge.
India: Markets respond to unfavorable government budget announcement.
Indonesia: Crash sparked by labor disputes and ethnic tensions.
Malaysia: Central bank hikes interest rates to curb inflation.
Poland: Resignation of finance minister amid scandal.
Mexico: Response to Colosio assassination and U.S. interest rate hikes.
S. Africa: Rumors surrounding first race-neutral general election held April 27, 1994.
Turkey: Political disagreements over economic austerity program introduced by Ciller government leads to devaluation of lira.
Venezuela: Finance minister resigns over loose monetary policy designed to avert growing domestic banking crisis.
Germany: Capital outflow in response to high U.S. interest rates and various real estate and bank scandals.

We answer this question by considering the extreme case in which all financial disturbances are country-specific, so that the data generating processes for the x_{it}--that is, the random events that determine movements in stock prices, exchange rates, and foreign reserves--are statistically independent across countries. This case is useful because it provides a lower bound for the probability of finding contemporaneous collapses that are idiosyncratic. Initially, let us also assume that the x_{it} are normally distributed.

Consider first a particular set of four countries, say, Brazil, Germany, Malaysia, and Poland.[15] Given the assumptions above, the probability that these particular four countries would simultaneously experience unrelated asset price collapses is very low: $(0.025)^4$. Therefore, if we had been looking for crisis episodes involving these four countries and found them, country-specific factors would have been unlikely to explain them. Our definition of a multicountry episode, however, picks out contemporaneous asset price collapses in *any* four countries out of the 23-country sample. In this way we significantly increase the probability of identifying a country-specific crisis episode, although at 3.5 percent it is still not high.

We suspect, however, that the x_{it} are not normally distributed. As we saw in Table 2.2, the sample distributions for stock prices and foreign reserves in particular appear to have fat tails. A relaxation of this assumption helps to explain the relatively high incidence of country-specific crises we identify: If independent crises occur 5 percent of the time instead of 2.5 percent of the time, the probability that a country-specific crisis episode occurs rises to 5.5 percent; if independent crises occur 10 percent of the time, the probability rises to 88.5 percent.

Of course, we also have reason to believe that the x_{it} are not independent. The average absolute stock price correlation between countries over the full sample period is 0.21; for some countries, such

[15] The choice of countries in this thought experiment is arbitrary. As defined here for normally distributed x_{it}, the probability of a collapse in any individual country is 0.025.

Table 2.4

Crisis Episodes Sorted by Hypothesized Causal Factor

Hypothesized Causal Factor	Episode Number	Date	Countries Affected
Common shock			
	2	June 1989	China, Hong Kong, Indonesia, Japan, Malaysia, Singapore
	5	Aug-Sept 1990	All countries?
Identified country-specific factors			
	4	Feb-April 1990	Argentina, Brazil, Taiwan, Germany, Japan
	6	Nov-Dec 1990	Hungary, Thailand
	7	March 1991	Argentina, Brazil
	8	July 1992	China, Mexico, Germany, Hong Kong
	9	Jan-June 1994	Chile, India, Indonesia, Malaysia, Poland, Mexico, South Africa, Turkey, Venezuela, Germany
Unidentified country-specific factors			
	1	March-April 1989	Argentina, Chile, Mexico, Philippines, Turkey
	2	June 1989	Argentina, Brazil, Chile
	4	Feb-April 1990	Argentina, Indonesia, Malaysia, Mexico, Taiwan, Turkey, Germany, Japan, Singapore, U.K.
	6	Nov-Dec 1990	Brazil, India, Poland, Turkey, Germany
	7	March 1991	Indonesia, Turkey, Japan, Singapore, U.S.
	9	Jan-June 1994	Hungary, Philippines, Hong Kong, Singapore, U.K., U.S.
	10	Jan-March 1995	Germany
Contagion			
	3	October 1989	Malaysia, Turkey, Germany, Singapore, U.K., U.S.
	10	Jan-March 1995	Argentina, Brazil, Chile, China, Czech Republic, Hungary, Malaysia, Mexico, Philippines, Poland, S. Africa, Turkey, Venezuela
	11	July-Aug 1997	Brazil, Indonesia, Malaysia, Philippines, Thailand, Germany, Singapore, U.S.

as Malaysia and Thailand, stock price correlations are greater than 50 percent. While these high correlations reflect the increasing international integration of stock and currency markets, and therefore their vulnerability to common shocks, it is difficult to assess the relevance of international financial integration to the probability of identifying country-specific crisis episodes. The distribution of common as well as country-specific shocks must be known before we can determine whether international financial market integration makes country-specific episodes more or less likely.[16]

We conclude, therefore, that country-specific factors can in theory reasonably explain many multicountry crisis episodes that might on the surface appear to be contagious. This suggests that, in many cases, external financial disturbances are poor excuses for public policy shortcomings. But it remains to distinguish which episodes are legitimately external in origin. We would like to find a more methodical way to distinguish between categories of multicountry crises than simply accepting the conclusions of market observers and analysts. In the next chapter, we propose a statistical methodology for testing hypotheses about the origins of multicountry crises.

[16] A simple model indicates the problem. Suppose that stock price movements in countries A and B evolve as follows:

$$dS^A_t = u^A_t + \alpha_{AB}u^B_t + v^A_t, \text{ and}$$
$$dS^B_t = \alpha_{BA}u^A_t + u^B_t + v^B_t;$$

where the v_t are random variables representing country-specific news events, the u_t are random variables representing systematic news events or common shocks, and the covariance parameters α_{AB} and α_{BA} are positive. Let the collapse boundaries for dS^A_t and dS^B_t be, respectively, σ_A and σ_B. If we wish to know the joint probability $P(dS^A_t < \sigma_A, dS^B_t < \sigma_B)$ when u^A_t and u^B_t are both zero (so that only country-specific news events are driving stock price movements), we need to know the distribution of both types of news events.

3. EMPIRICAL ANALYSIS

Our empirical analysis covers four of the eleven crisis events identified in Table 2.3:

- August-September 1990 Gulf War crisis (episode 5)
- January-June 1994 crisis (episode 9)
- January-March 1995 Mexican peso crisis (episode 10)
- July-August 1997 Thai baht crisis (episode 11).

We choose these four episodes on the basis of the evidence provided by news accounts and official reports. Our starting-out assumptions are that they represent, respectively,

- a global stock market crash due to the common shock of the Gulf War (episode 5)
- a set of country-specific crises, perhaps magnified by increases in U.S. interest rates (episode 9)
- financial contagion in EMC stock and currency markets triggered by Mexico's devaluation of the peso (episode 10)
- financial contagion in EMC stock and currency markets triggered by Thailand's devaluation of the baht (episode 11).

For any given multicountry episode, if country-specific factors are solely responsible for each country's crisis, we would expect to reject statistically the hypothesis of a causal relationship between an external trigger variable and local financial variables. In the case of contagion or a common shock, however, we would expect lags of the external trigger variable to help predict movements in local financial variables. Consider, for example, the case of a Philippine stock market crash. If the crash were caused by an attempted coup (as was probably the case in December 1989), the probability of finding a relationship between, say, movements in the Thai baht and Philippine stock prices should be low. However, if the crash were caused by a devaluation of the Thai baht, lagged movements in the baht should help predict stock price movements during the crisis period. Thus we would not expect to reject the null hypothesis of no causality with respect to the baht for Philippine stock price movements that occurred in December 1989, but we might expect to reject the null if we are examining Philippine stock price movements that took place during the crisis of July-August 1997.

We construct two types of causality tests: single-country tests employing single-equation time-series regression techniques and multicountry tests employing vector-autoregressions. With the first type of test, we look for evidence that sudden, sharp movements in an external financial variable triggered crises in the countries that experienced them during the episode being examined. The second type of test, or block causality test, allows us to see whether groups of countries were generally responsive to the trigger variables we select.

Because the Mexican peso and Thai baht crises appear to have had a strong regional dimension, we group the East Asian and Latin American EMCs by region. Remaining EMCs are grouped into a "loner" category, while the more developed markets are grouped into a "financial center" category. In order to see whether the nature of possible causal relationships changed during the crisis, we test for causality over the full sample period as well as a 24-month period spanning each crisis episode.[17]

Statistical causality tests allow us to examine the strength of lead and lag relationships without a formal structural economic model. Upon testing for the optimal lead and lag structure, we choose a symmetric structure of four leads and four lags.[18] We report F-tests

---

[17] The crisis period window, arbitrarily chosen to be 24 months, is always centered on the crisis episode, except in the case of the Thai baht crisis. (In that case, for data reasons, the crisis episode occurs at the end of the window.) Note that the full sample period contains each of the crisis episodes, so that we are not able to make a strict crisis- versus non-crisis-period comparison.

[18] The equation we estimate using the Geweke-Meese-Dent (1982) single equation causality test procedure is

$$x_{it} = \alpha + \sum\beta_k z_{t+k} + u_t; \; k = \{-4, \ldots, 4\}$$

and chi-square significance values for the single-country and regional causality tests; starred values indicate that the null hypothesis of zero coefficients on the trigger variable at all lags can be rejected at either a 5- or 10-percent level of confidence. The results are presented in Tables 3.1 through 3.4.

For the crises that occurred during August and September of 1990, an obvious explanation is that current or projected oil price increases stemming from the onset of the Gulf War sparked widespread declines in national stock markets. Lacking weekly spot or forward market data on oil prices, we instead test an alternative hypothesis that falling U.S. stock prices were responsible for the worldwide stock market declines.

The evidence, summarized in Table 3.1, is mixed. Overall, we find that lagged U.S. stock price movements did not trigger most of the stock market crises that occurred during the crisis subperiod. For financial center stock markets as a group, however, U.S. stock market movements appear to have been influential during the 24 months surrounding the crisis episode, as they do for individual stock markets in Turkey and Hong Kong.

A similar exercise is conducted with respect to the January-June 1994 crisis (hereafter referred to as "episode 9"), which we believe may have been a series of idiosyncratic stock market collapses in 13 individual countries. The results of the exercise are summarized in Table 3.2. Because U.S. interest rate increases are reported to have been a factor in several of the countries' stock market declines, we

---

where x_{it} is the stock price or exchange rate for each country in crisis as defined above, α is a constant term, z_t is the hypothesized external financial trigger variable, u_t is a random error term, and k indexes the lead and lag structure. The joint null hypothesis is that $\beta_k = 0$ for $k = \{-4, \ldots, -1\}$.

For regional tests involving stock price or exchange rate movements in N countries, the VAR system estimated is

$$Y_t = A_0 + \sum A_k Y_{t-k} + \sum B_k z_{t-k} + U_t; \; k = \{1, \ldots, 4\}$$

where Y_t and U_t are N by 1 vectors, A_0 is an N by 1 vector of intercepts, A_k is an N by N matrix of coefficients, B_k is an N by 1 vector of coefficients, and z_t and k are as defined above. The joint null hypothesis is that $B_k = 0$ for all i and k.

once again test the alternative hypothesis that U.S. stock market declines--proxying for U.S. interest rate increases--were really responsible for the collapses that took place over the crisis period. Here, the result is unambiguous: We cannot reject the null hypothesis of causality for any individual country or country grouping, either during the 24 months surrounding the crisis or over the full sample period.

For the Gulf War episode and episode 9, we use proxies for the trigger variables suggested in the financial press: world oil prices and U.S. short-term interest rates.[19] But the clear starting hypothesis for the Mexican peso crisis episode of January-March 1995 is that the fall of the peso was responsible for both stock- and currency-market collapses in the EMCs identified in Table 2.3. We therefore examine movements in both stock and currency markets, defining movement in the Mexican peso/U.S. dollar rate as the triggering event. As shown in Table 3.3, some surprising patterns emerge. On the regional front, stock and currency markets in the Asian EMCs and financial centers, but not in Latin America, appear to have been affected by crisis-period events in Mexico. For individual countries, lagged movements in the Mexican peso/dollar exchange rate appear to have influenced currency values but not stock prices in Argentina, Chile, and the Philippines during the 24 months surrounding the crisis episode.[20] This is surprising because the majority of the collapses we identify during this episode, including those in Chile and the Philippines, are stock price collapses.[21] Nevertheless, the pattern appears to be consistent with a

---

[19] An interesting extension to this research would be to collect weekly spot oil price and U.S. interest data and redo the causality tests with these as trigger variables.

[20] For Argentina, the currency crisis was manifested in sharp declines in foreign exchange reserves. Although the value of the Argentine peso remained within a 0.2 percent band around its U.S. dollar parity peg during the 24 month crisis period window, the movements that occurred within that band appear to have been "caused" by movements in the Mexican peso.

[21] A closer inspection of our estimated equation reveals that contemporaneous, as opposed to lagged, movements in the Mexican peso do have strong explanatory power for stock price movements in Argentina, Brazil, and Chile. This suggests that our failure to reject the hypothesis of no statistical causality for these countries may be an artifact of our weekly data.

story of contagion spreading from Mexico to other EMCs in Latin America and in East Asia.

For the final crisis we examine (the Thai baht crisis of July-August 1997), we follow a procedure similar to that followed for Mexico. The baht/U.S. dollar rate is defined as the external trigger variable. As shown in Table 3.4, the evidence is consistent with press reports indicating that currency market turbulence in Thailand influenced both stock and currency market movements in Indonesia, Malaysia, and the Philippines during the 24 months leading up to the crisis. In fact, for the Asian EMCs as a whole, we can reject the null hypothesis of causality with at least 10 percent confidence for the full sample period as well as the subperiod containing the crisis episode. More surprising, it appears that movements in the baht/U.S. dollar exchange rate also caused movements in financial center exchange rates, and specifically in the German mark/U.S. dollar, Singapore dollar/U.S. dollar, and U.S. dollar/SDR exchange rates. One possible explanation for the Singapore and U.S. dollar results is that both the baht and the Singapore dollar were tightly pegged to the U.S. dollar over most of the period.[22]

Summary of Findings

Overall, our results support the popular wisdom that contagion, or loss of confidence in local financial assets due to a foreign financial collapse, was a greater factor in the Mexican and Thai crises than in the first two crisis episodes. But there are some important limitations to the statistical methodology we use. First, the causality results apply only to the trigger variable specified in the empirical estimation. If the wrong trigger variable is chosen and the equation misspecified, a crisis might wrongly be classified as country specific. We believe this to be a minor limitation because the triggering events

---

[22] This explanation is supported by an independent causality test on the U.S.-dollar-pegged Hong Kong dollar, which despite never actually experiencing a collapse, nevertheless appears also to have been influenced by movements in the baht during both the full sample period and crisis subperiod.

for multicountry crises labeled as common-shock or contagious crisis episodes are by definition clearly identified.

Second, the methodology could be sensitive to the frequency of the available data and the length of the crisis window. For example, if a global political crisis such as the Gulf War were to create panic in Thai currency markets the day before affecting Malaysian stock markets, tests on daily data might wrongly attribute Malaysian stock market declines to a decline in the Thai baht. On the other hand, weekly data will miss large and legitimate international market interactions that are likely to occur at higher frequencies during a crisis. For example, a Wednesday drop in the Mexican peso may encourage investors to dump Venezuelan stocks on Thursday, but this relationship will not be captured by tests on weekly data. With respect to the length of the crisis window, a longer window provides more degrees of freedom for statistical estimation, but also tends to dilute those relationships that exist only during the crisis itself.[23] While we believe that the first and third problems are relatively minor in our case, the second problem may be more significant.

Finally, and most important from a policy standpoint, these simple statistical techniques tell us little about underlying economic conditions in the countries that experience collapses, or about the mechanisms by which disturbances are transmitted between countries. For example, they allow us to identify collapses that appear to have been exogenous to particular external events, but do not tell us the extent to which local economic conditions may have contributed to externally triggered collapses. They also do not tell us why some countries were vulnerable to externally generated crises while others were not. These issues, therefore, will be the focus of the next two chapters.

---

[23] In fact, our results are largely robust to the choice between a 12-month and 24-month window length. Large movements in the x_{it} during the crisis episode itself tend to dominate.

Table 3.1

Significance Levels for Causality and Block Causality Tests: U.S. Stocks as Trigger for Gulf War Period Stock Market Crashes

Country or Country Group	January 1989 - August 1997	September 1989 - September 1991
Regional Country Groupings		
East Asian EMCs[a]	0.487	0.170
Latin American EMCs[b]	0.567	0.161
"Loner" EMCs[c]	0.642	na
Financial Centers[d]	0.249	0.060*
Individual Markets		
Malaysia	0.299	0.574
Mexico	0.958	0.713
Philippines	0.271	0.611
Taiwan	0.523	0.440
Turkey	0.434	0.079*
Germany	0.393	0.248
Hong Kong	0.358	0.097*
Japan	0.577	0.716
Singapore	0.819	0.874
United Kingdom	0.382	0.433

NOTE: * Can reject null hypothesis of causality with 10 percent confidence.

** Can reject null hypothesis of causality with 5 percent confidence.

[a]Asian EMCs include Indonesia, Malaysia, Philippines, Taiwan, and Thailand. Data begin October 5, 1990, and end August 22, 1997.

[b]Latin American EMCs include Argentina, Brazil, Chile, Mexico, and Venezuela. Data begin January 6, 1989, and end August 22, 1997.

[c]"Loner" EMCs include Hungary, India, Poland, South Africa, and Turkey. Data begin January 8, 1993, and end October 18, 1996. The Czech Republic is omitted due to the shortness of the data sample.

[d]Financial centers include Germany, Hong Kong, Japan, Singapore, the United Kingdom, and the United States.

Table 3.2

Significance Levels for Causality and Block Causality Tests: U.S. Stocks as Trigger for Episode 9 Stock Market Crashes

Country or Country Group	January 1989 - August 1997	April 1993 - April 1995
Regional Country Groupings		
East Asian EMCs[a]	0.487	0.746
Latin American EMCs	0.567	0.988
"Loner" EMCs[b]	0.642	0.207
Financial Centers	0.249	0.777
Individual Markets		
Chile	0.703	0.551
Hungary[b]	0.911	0.774
India	0.284	0.875
Malaysia	0.299	0.402
Philippines	0.271	0.172
Poland[b]	0.226	0.147
South Africa[b]	0.445	0.627
Turkey	0.434	0.919
Venezuela	0.495	0.336
Germany	0.393	0.953
Hong Kong	0.358	0.526
Singapore	0.819	0.208
United Kingdom	0.382	0.678

NOTE: For country groupings, see notes to Table 3.1.
* Can reject null hypothesis of causality with 10 percent confidence.
** Can reject null hypothesis of causality with 5 percent confidence
[a]Does not include China.
[b]Data begin January 8, 1993, and end October 18, 1996.

Table 3.3

Significance Levels for Causality and Block Causality Tests: Mexican Peso as Trigger for Mexican Peso Crisis Period Turbulence

Country or Country Group	January 1989 - August 1997		March 1994 - March 1996	
	Stock Prices	Exchange Rates	Stock Prices	Exchange Rates
Regional Country Groupings				
East Asian EMCs[a]	0.115	0.036**	0.026**	0.000**
Latin American EMCs	0.219	0.997	0.515	0.806
"Loner" EMCs[b]	0.329	0.993	0.263	0.998
Financial Centers	0.239	0.368	0.026**	0.000**
Individual Markets				
Argentina	0.872	0.821	0.160	0.017**
Brazil	0.570	0.430	0.450	0.783
Chile	0.027**	0.001**	0.151	0.002**
China[b]	0.662	0.989	0.696	0.989
Hungary[b]	0.491	0.951	0.451	0.951
Malaysia	0.404	0.855	0.441	0.582
Philippines	0.789	0.374	0.399	0.002**
Poland[b]	0.544	0.880	0.364	0.808
South Africa[b]	0.170	0.374	0.143	0.426
Turkey	0.564	0.687	0.861	0.877
Venezuela	0.368	0.952	0.557	0.986

NOTE: For country groupings, see notes to Table 3.1.

* Can reject null hypothesis of causality with 10 percent confidence.

** Can reject null hypothesis of causality with 5 percent confidence.

[a]Does not include China.

[b]Data begin January 8, 1993, and end October 18, 1996.

Table 3.4

Significance Levels for Causality and Block Causality Tests: Thai Baht as Trigger for Thai Baht Crisis Period Turbulence

	January 1989 - August 1997		August 1995 - August 1997	
Country or Country Group	Stock Prices	Exchange Rates	Stock Prices	Exchange Rates
Regional Country Groupings				
East Asian EMCs[a]	0.490	0.000**	0.023**	0.000**
Latin American EMCs	0.288	0.999	0.125	0.982
"Loner" EMCs[b]	0.000**	0.998	na	na
Financial Centers	0.148	0.061*	0.021**	0.079*
Individual Markets				
Brazil	0.926	0.407	0.587	0.386
Indonesia[c]	0.331	0.121	0.075*	0.000**
Malaysia	0.616	0.335	0.012**	0.014**
Philippines	0.315	0.540	0.058*	0.000**
Germany	0.071*	0.000**	0.356	0.346
Singapore	0.560	0.034**	0.810	0.805
United States	0.276	0.001**	0.936	0.931

NOTE: For country groupings see notes to Table 3.1.

* Can reject null hypothesis of causality with 10 percent confidence.

** Can reject null hypothesis of causality with 5 percent confidence.

[a]Does not include China.

[b]Data begin January 8, 1993, and end October 18, 1996.

[c]Data begin October 5, 1990.

4. FOUR INFORMAL MODELS OF FINANCIAL CONTAGION

We have argued above that there are many reasons why several countries might experience financial crises at the same, or close to the same, time. The possible explanations include coincidental shocks affecting financial conditions in individual countries, a common shock to fundamental economic conditions across countries, and financial contagion, where contagion is broadly defined to be a causal relationship between national financial crises. These explanations are not mutually exclusive, and as we have seen, it can be difficult to distinguish empirically between them using broad-brush statistical techniques. An alternative approach is to examine more carefully the nature of the crisis-transmission mechanism. This approach provides an added benefit because different transmission mechanisms have different policy implications.

Table 4.1 presents four models of financial contagion and summarizes their implications for the predictability and preventability of downstream crises. According to the economic-linkages model, one country's financial crisis precipitates a crisis in downstream economies by changing their economic fundamentals. This is essentially a special case of the common-shock explanation for multicountry crises, in which the external shock is a financial event overseas. Formalizations of this model include Gerlach and Smets (1994), and Huh and Kasa (1997). An example is a forced currency devaluation that affects other countries' terms of trade. Once the initial crisis has occurred, the pattern of downstream crises should be relatively easy to predict as trade patterns are well-known and rather slow to change. However, it is not so obvious what the affected countries could or should do to prevent them--other than to make policy adjustments as soon as possible in order to realign their fundamentals with the new situation.

The second model, heightened awareness, combines information gaps with weak (but unchanged) fundamentals. Here we posit that data and analysis for individual emerging markets are either of poor quality or expensive for investors to acquire. Because they do not or cannot collect the data relevant to all of the countries in their portfolios, diversified investors focus on just a few.[24] When these countries get into trouble, investors take a closer look at the other countries whose assets make up their portfolios and do not like what they see. They therefore try to sell off assets from this second tier of countries as well. This model is closely related to the herd-behavior model described below. The key distinction, however, is that in a heightened-awareness world, the countries that experience crises generally do have poor fundamentals. Those with problems that look similar to the first country's problems, or that have gaps in their reporting, are most vulnerable to downstream contagion. Better reporting and analysis of relevant data could reduce exposure to contagion by reducing the cost of information, but better policies would be even more effective.

Table 4.1

Four Models of Financial Contagion and Implications for Downstream Economies

Transmission Mechanisms for Contagious Crises	Predictability of Crisis Downstream	Preventability of Crisis Downstream
Economic-Linkages Model Crisis in first country affects fundamentals of other countries	Good	Poor
Heightened-Awareness Model Crisis in first country reveals possibly poor fundamentals in other countries	Fair	Good
Portfolio-Adjustment Model Crisis in first country forces technical realignment of investor portfolios	Good	Poor
Herd-Behavior Model Crisis in first country induces herd behavior by investors	Poor	Fair

[24] Calvo and Mendoza (1996) show that incomplete collection of expensive information can be optimal when investors are diversified.

In the portfolio-adjustment model, liquidity-constrained portfolio managers need cash to meet the expected increase in redemptions of the original crisis country's assets. They respond by selling the assets of other countries included in the portfolio. This triggers a second set of crises in these countries. To the extent that portfolio managers consistently group countries into portfolios according to geographic location, the potential for predicting this sort of contagion is good. Further, among the most vulnerable to this type of contagion should be countries with large foreign debts packaged into regional debt portfolios, because such portfolios are often highly leveraged through offshore derivative instruments.[25] However, as portfolio composition is determined institutionally, over time geographic location may no longer be a useful predictor of downstream vulnerability.

Finally, in the herd-behavior model, investors create downstream contagion by abandoning certain of their portfolio investments in response to what they think other investors are doing. In contrast to the heightened-awareness model, economic fundamentals need not be weak in order for investors to panic.[26] If investors are mostly unsophisticated small retail investors, the potential for prediction in this case is fair: A country's popularity with retail investors will be a strong indicator of its vulnerability to contagion.[27] Steps to discourage retail investment until financial markets and their regulatory and reporting systems are well established could reduce the likelihood of contagion, but would at the same time reduce some "good"

[25] The problem may be aggravated if tightly regulated onshore derivatives markets motivate borrowers to go offshore. In this situation, EMC policymakers may have a very imperfect understanding of the true dimensions of their outstanding foreign currency debt. Garber and Lall (1996) argue that largely unregulated offshore derivatives markets exacerbated the turbulence of Mexican currency markets in January–March 1995.

[26] There is evidence for this model in both stock and currency markets. See for example Calvo and Reinhart (1996), Eichengreen, Rose, and Wyplosz (1995), and Wolf (1996).

[27] It is not clear whether mutual funds tend to behave more like retail investors or institutional investors in this context. During the Mexico crisis, anecdotal evidence suggests that mutual fund managers sold off assets in anticipation of redemptions by individual investors; apparently those redemptions never materialized.

investment as well. It is not clear, moreover, that such panics are limited to unsophisticated investors. Recent empirical research suggests that reacting to unsubstantiated rumors may be quite rational when information is incomplete or costly to acquire.[28] If so, this type of contagion is not limited to retail investors, and may be impossible to predict. However, reducing the cost of information will once again be an important preventive step.

Traditional Indicators of Vulnerability to Crises[29]

Traditional economic indicators of a country's vulnerability to stock market crashes and currency crises can be grouped into two categories: macroeconomic and political developments that shake the confidence of investors, and structural characteristics of the market that make it vulnerable to such losses of investor confidence. A nonexhaustive list of these indicators is presented in Table 4.2. If crises are caused by poor government policies over time, both kinds of indicators should help to explain *why* crises occur. But because structural indicators tend to be slow to change, macroeconomic developments are more useful for predicting *when* crises will occur.

All else equal, we might expect domestic stock markets to be most sensitive to developments that threaten the profitability of domestic industries, while currency markets are vulnerable to developments that threaten a central bank's ability or willingness to maintain the value of the domestic currency and, thus, the value of domestic-currency-denominated asset returns. Clearly many developments will be equally damaging to stock prices and the value of the currency—falling export growth, for example, or an increasing real exchange rate. But the rapid money supply and domestic credit growth that fuels stock market booms puts downward pressure on the domestic currency, while the high interest rates needed to defend sagging currencies take the luster off of equity investments. High and rising unemployment may signal a country's

---

[28] See, for example, Scharfstein and Stein (1990), Banerjee (1992), and Calvo and Mendoza (1996).

[29] An exhaustive survey of currency crisis indicators is presented in Kaminsky, Lizondo, and Reinhart (1997).

Table 4.2

Traditional Economic Indicators of Financial Vulnerability

Macroeconomic Developments	Structural Characteristics
High and rising inflation rate	Rigid exchange rate regime
Rapid money supply growth	Export-led growth strategy
Falling real export growth	Highly concentrated export sector
High and rising fiscal deficit	High variable-rate component of external debt
Increasing real exchange rate relative to trend	High short-term component of external debt
Rapid domestic credit growth as a percentage of GDP	Recent financial market liberalization
High and rising proportion of nonperforming loans to total loans	Poor financial regulatory/supervisory framework
Rising current account deficit as a percentage of GDP	Credit markets collateralized by real or financial assets
Large and growing foreign-currency-denominated external debt	Low stock market capitalization
Falling international reserves	Stock market dominated by few firms
Falling real economic growth	Stock market dominated by few industries
High and rising price/earnings ratio	Controls on market entry and exit
Rising domestic interest rates	
High and rising unemployment rate	

SOURCE: Eichengreen, Rose, and Wyplosz (1995); Frankel and Rose (1996); Kaminsky and Reinhart (1996); Sachs, Tornell, and Velasco (1996).

unwillingness to sacrifice economic growth for an exchange rate objective.

Structurally, small and highly concentrated stock markets tend to be most sensitive to changes in economic conditions as well as fluctuating investor sentiments. Exchange rates in countries that depend largely on short-term portfolio capital inflows to fund domestic investment may be more vulnerable to attack than exchange rates in countries in which foreign direct investment plays a larger role.[30] A large external debt also contributes to investor nervousness about the stability of the exchange rate, especially when the debt is composed largely of short-term and variable-rate instruments. In general, fixed and heavily managed exchange rate regimes are likely to provide the greatest lure to currency speculators. Governments that experiment with capital controls worry stock and currency market participants alike.

Unfortunately, we know of no studies that use out-of-sample forecasting techniques to test how well these traditional indicators predict the various types of financial crises in EMCs.[31] Several studies, however, have looked at the within-sample explanatory power of various currency crisis indicators. Although there are some differences in results, depending on the estimation methodology used, recent research suggests that movements in international reserves, export performance, real economic growth, domestic credit, domestic inflation, and movements in the real exchange rate are among the most useful predictors of currency crises in developed as well as emerging market countries (Kaminsky, Lizondo, and Reinhart, 1997). We appear to know far less, however, about the determinants of stock market crashes.

Contagion indicators

Even countries that exhibit few of the traditional indicators of financial vulnerability listed in Table 4.2 may have reason to worry about externally generated financial contagion. We demonstrate this

[30] Evidence for the high sensitivity of portfolio capital inflows to disturbances is presented in Chuhan, Perez-Quiros, and Popper (1997).

[31] Meese and Rose (1996) do examine the out-of-sample predictability of exchange rate crashes for eight members of the European monetary system.

point by examining the behavior of a set of traditional crisis indicators for the four Southeast Asian EMCs. For comparison purposes, we choose calendar year 1994 (prior to the fallout from the Mexican peso collapse) and calendar year 1996 (prior to the fallout from the Thai baht collapse) as our reference time periods.

Table 4.3

Value of Crisis Indicators Before Mexico and Before Thailand: Southeast Asian EMCs (percentages)

Indicator	Indonesia		Malaysia		Philippines		Thailand	
	1994	1996	1994	1996	1994	1996	1994	1996
Real GDP growth	7.5	7.8	9.2	8.2	4.4	5.5	8.7	6.7
Unemployment rate	2.8	7.2	3.0	3.0	8.4	7.4	1.3	2.0
Export growth[a]	9.9	9.7	23.1	7.0	18.5	17.7	22.1	-1.9
Current account/GDP	-1.6	-3.5	-6.4	-5.2	-4.6	-4.3	-5.6	-7.9
Real exchange appreciation[c]	2.3	2.3	1.3	1.9	10.4	4.9	3.1	1.1
Inflation[b]	8.0	8.5	5.5	4.4	10.0	8.9	4.6	4.8
M2 growth	20.2	29.6	14.7	21.4	26.8	15.8	12.9	12.6
Domestic credit as percentage of GDP	20.5	23.0	76.1	93.3	48.5	68.8	91.7	99.3
Percentage of loans that are nonperforming	12.0	8.8	8.1	3.9	4.2	3.3	7.5	na
International reserves[d]	19.7	22.1	22.2	17.9	13.9	15.3	28.0	26.7

SOURCES: Asia Development Bank, International Monetary Fund, Bank for International Settlements, Bank Negara Malaysia, Bangko Central ng Pilipinas.

NOTE: All growth rates measured as percentage change over previous year.
[a]Percent change in U.S. dollar value of merchandise exports
[b]Percent change in GDP deflator
[c]Nominal exchange rate less inflation differential with U.S.
[d]Measured as weeks of imports

As shown in Table 4.3, excepting Thailand itself, there was no consistent pattern of economic or financial deterioration for the Southeast Asian EMCs during the three years prior to the series of speculative attacks that resulted in the July 1997 collapse of the Thai baht. In fact, many of the 1996 indicators for Indonesia, Malaysia, and the Philippines suggested economies that were still booming. In Malaysia, for example, despite a decline in economic growth between 1994 and 1996, the 1996 growth rate was 8.2 percent. In the Philippines, the majority of the indicators suggest that economic performance actually improved over the period. There were signs of a possible overextension of credit in all four countries, but the only consistent indications of trouble to come were in Thailand.

Yet, in sharp contrast to their fairly mild experience of the multicountry Mexican peso crisis, currency and stock markets in Indonesia, Malaysia, and the Philippines suffered collateral damage from troubles in Thailand even before the baht's eventual collapse in July 1997.[32] Was this predictable? Based on the indicators listed above, it was not. On the basis of our four contagion models, however, Table 4.4 presents an additional set of conditions that we believe indicated these countries' vulnerability to downstream contagion from Thailand. In the next chapter we present three short case studies that provide initial, informal evidence of the validity of these contagion models and predictors.

---

[32] Indonesian, Malaysian, and Thai currency markets were in turmoil during the week of January 9-13, 1995. Periodic pressure against the Philippine peso continued into late March.

Table 4.4

Conditions Indicating Vulnerability to Financial Contagion

Contagion Indicator	Applicable to: Stock Crises	Currency Crises
Economic Linkages		
Strong economic links to country experiencing crisis	X	X
Highly competitive with country experiencing crisis	X	X
Heightened Awareness		
Similar fundamentals to country experiencing crisis		X
Financial or political skeletons in the closet	X	X
Poor or incomplete economic data or analysis available to investors	X	X
Portfolio Adjustment		
Consistently member of portfolios containing crisis country	X	X
Capital inflows highly leveraged	X	X
Herd Behavior		
Market experienced dramatic capital inflow in past	X	X
Market dominated by retail investors and mutual funds	X	X

5. THE EVOLUTION OF FINANCIAL CRISES: THREE CASE STUDIES

The three case studies we choose represent three different types of financial crises and three different experiences with contagion. The first case, Argentina during the Mexican crisis of 1994-1995, is a contagion story that illustrates the centrality of a healthy banking system to investor confidence. The second case, which describes South Africa's difficulties in 1996, offers a counterpoint to the Argentine case: a currency crisis with a healthy banking system and no contagion. The last case is perhaps the most worrisome: Thailand's troubles, by no means ended with the devaluation and subsequent partial floating of the baht on July 2, 1997, have developed into a full-blown contagious financial crisis in Asia.

Case Study 1: Argentina[33]

The Mexican peso crisis of late 1994 and early 1995 had major repercussions for Argentine financial markets. With a weak financial system, an inflexible exchange rate regime, and a heavy reliance on short-term foreign capital inflows, Argentina exhibited many of the indicators of vulnerability discussed in the previous chapter. The results were unfortunate. As in Mexico, Argentine stock and bond markets suffered huge losses, capital fled the country, the central bank lost substantial international reserves, and the Argentine banking system experienced serious liquidity problems. Many small and medium banks became insolvent.

Prior to the crisis, the Argentine economy seemed to be doing well. Between 1991 and 1994, GDP grew at an annual average rate of 7.7 percent. Inflation had fallen from a peak rate of 20,266 percent in March 1990 to an average of just 3.9 percent in 1994. Capital outflows, which during the 1980s reached over $150 billion, had become capital

---

33 Unless otherwise specified, the economic statistics presented in this section come from the Ministry of Economy and Public Works (1995).

inflows as $25 billion of foreign investment flowed in between 1990 and 1993 alone. In 1993, Argentina ranked fifth among emerging markets in attracting foreign investment flows, ranked only behind Mexico, Malaysia, China, and Thailand (IMF, *International Financial Statistics*, various issues).[34]

The significant policy shift behind this economic improvement was the Convertibility Plan implemented in April 1991. The heart of the plan was a 1:1 peg of the Argentine peso to the U.S. dollar. To support the peg, the plan established a currency board and prohibited monetarization of public budget deficits. It also allowed Argentine residents to open foreign currency bank accounts. However, it made no provision for reform of the banking sector, which, as in so many EMCs, had a number of poorly managed state banks, lacked adequate supervision over all banks, and did not have deposit insurance.[35]

Effects of the Mexican Peso Crisis on Argentine Financial Markets

The sharp devaluation of the Mexican peso on December 20, 1994, had immediate and devastating consequences for the Argentine financial system. One theory, which corresponds to the heightened awareness model of Table 4.1, is that similarities between the economies of Argentina and Mexico caused investors to fear that events in Mexico would be repeated in Argentina. The result was a crisis of confidence in Argentine financial markets, leading to a sharp decline in Argentina's international reserves, a huge sell-off of stocks and bonds, and a massive withdrawal of both Argentine peso- and U.S. dollar-denominated bank deposits.

To restore confidence and reduce speculative pressure on the peso, the central bank maintained its strong commitment to the Convertibility Plan. Nevertheless, dollarization continued to increase as investors' expectations of devaluation grew in January and February of 1995.

---

[34] Foreign investment inflow measures do not include Saudi Arabia, which is a special case.

[35] Lindgren, Garcia, and Saal (1996) argue that prudential regulations were in fact comprehensive, but that the supervisory agency lacked resources to keep up with banking-sector growth. Deposit insurance was eliminated in 1989 and was not reinstated until April 1995.

Between December 23, 1994, and March 31, 1995, the central bank lost US$5.5 billion of its international reserves due to panic conversion of pesos to dollars by the private sector. This represented more than one-third of its supply of liquid international reserves (IMF, 1996).

The panic also affected the stock market. Between December 19 and 31, 1994, Argentina's Merval stock price index dropped 12.4 percent. It fell a further 5.4 percent in January 1995, and experienced its largest drop in February, with a decline of 25.7 percent. At its lowest level in early March, it had fallen more than 50 percent from its peak on December 19. The market capitalization of the companies listed on the Buenos Aires Stock Exchange fell from 36.5 billion pesos on December 31, 1994 to 25.5 billion pesos at the end of February 1995, a 30 percent decline.

The financial crisis hit the Argentine banking system especially hard. A run on deposits generated liquidity problems for many banks, but the constraints of the exchange rate peg dissuaded the central bank from taking any strong measures to expand the money supply. Medium and small banks were especially vulnerable, with several provincial banks, cooperatives, and wholesale banks becoming insolvent.[36] Between December 20 and the end of March 1995, the banking system as a whole lost total deposits of about $7.5 billion (in both local and foreign currency), a reduction of 17 percent from the December 1994 level of $45.3 billion. The greatest losses occurred in the first few days of March 1995.

As a result of the 1994-1995 banking crisis, the Argentine banking system was restructured and consolidated. In all, the crisis caused a loss of deposits worth $8 billion. This amount was covered by a $4 billion fall in the central bank's international reserves, a $2 billion decline in banking system liquidity, a $1 billion contraction in loans, and a $1 billion foreign loan (Caprio and Klingebiel 1996).

---

[36] In all, the IMF reports that the number of Argentine financial institutions fell by 25 percent between December 1994 and March 1996 (IMF, 1996, p. 113).

Lessons from the Argentine Crisis

Why were Argentine financial markets so vulnerable to contagion from Mexico? A weak banking system must form part of the answer. These four factors may have contributed to the poor showing of Argentina's banks during the crisis:

- heavy government involvement in banking
- high proportion of nonperforming loans
- lack of public trust in the banking sector
- weakness in bank accounting and disclosure frameworks.

Heavy government involvement in banking, which takes the form of direct ownership of banks, means that Argentine banks generally operate without much autonomy. As a result, they tend to be inefficient and commercially imprudent in lending: Loans are generally not based on creditworthiness but, rather, on political connections and government priorities. As a result, in December 1994 the entire Argentine banking system was overloaded with nonperforming loans. Slightly over 10 percent of private bank loans were nonperforming, while in public banks, the proportion was closer to 30 percent of total loan assets.[37]

Further, a long history of hyperinflation has created a deep and persistent distrust of bank deposits among many Argentines. Total bank deposits amount to 20 percent of GDP, just half the level that prevails in much smaller Chile (Caprio and Klingebiel, 1996). Lack of confidence in the Argentine banking system was one of the main reasons behind the sudden withdrawal of deposits during the crisis.

Finally, in December 1994, Argentina had not yet adopted international bank accounting standards. Rules on disclosure of bad loans were not clearly defined, making it hard to estimate accurately the magnitude of nonperforming loans. Lack of transparency and poor information also made it difficult for the central bank to monitor the operations of financial institutions.

---

[37] One reviewer has pointed out that private-sector banks are more than capable of making their own poor lending decisions. He cites the experience of private banks in Chile (1979-1982) and Mexico (1992-1994).

Relevance of Contagion Indicators

Although there is little evidence for the economic-linkages model, the other three models of financial contagion appear to be relevant in this case.

Heightened awareness. The crisis in its much larger Latin neighbor, Mexico, may have served to focus attention on existing financial problems in Argentina, and especially the vulnerability of its banking system. Investors suspected that, should there be a run on the peso, Argentine authorities would be unwilling to defend the peso/U.S. dollar parity peg and risk triggering a massive banking sector collapse. In the end, the authorities proved both willing and able to absorb the large banking sector losses (and the resulting depressing effects on economic growth) in order to preserve the dollar peg.

Portfolio adjustment. Argentina probably also suffered from the disadvantage of almost always being grouped with Mexico in regional investment portfolios. At the end of 1994 there were just five Argentina country funds with net assets of approximately $100 million operating at the end of 1994, as compared to 108 Latin America regional funds with net assets of almost $11 billion (IMF, 1993).

Herd behavior. Although not quite as popular an investment destination as Mexico, in 1993 Argentina ranked fifth among emerging markets in attracting foreign investment flows, ranked behind only Mexico, Malaysia, China, and Thailand. Retail investment made up a large part of the total. In contrast to the heightened-awareness story, it may be that investors were well aware of problems in the Argentine banking sector but were unwilling to be the first out of the market until Mexico collapsed, at which point they all moved together.

Case Study 2: South Africa[38]

In mid-February 1996, South Africa experienced a sharp depreciation of its currency, the rand, which had been relatively stable over the

---

[38] Unless otherwise specified, the economic statistics presented in this section come from the South African Reserve Bank (1996).

previous three years (Stals, 1996b). According to the South African Reserve Bank, the initial decline in the value of the rand was triggered by "unsubstantiated rumors" about the health of President Nelson Mandela and about an imminent relaxation or even abolition of all exchange controls by the central bank. According to the Governor of the Reserve Bank, South Africa's financial integration into the "global village . . . exposed [South Africa] to the whims of international investors" (Stals, 1996a).

It seems clear, nevertheless, that a low level of foreign exchange reserves, rapid expansion of domestic credit, and a growing current account deficit also contributed to investors' lack of confidence in the rand. February's initial depreciation was followed by large speculative capital outflows in March and April. From February 13 to February 29 the nominal effective exchange rate of the rand declined by 5.4 percent; between February 29 and July 31 it fell another 13 percent. Over the February–June period, a total of R4.6 billion of short-term capital fled the country, reflecting investors' declining confidence in South African financial markets.

As in Argentina, the period leading up to the crisis had been one of economic recovery. Political and social reforms in South Africa brought with them the termination of international sanctions and trade boycotts, and the beginnings of reintegration into the world economy. The rate of growth of GDP climbed from –2.2 percent in 1992 to 3.3 percent in 1995. Strong gains in private fixed investment provided the main stimulus to the expansion, growing at rates of 6.7 percent in 1994 and 5.6 percent in 1995. Nevertheless, the unemployment rate continued to increase, by some estimates reaching 33 percent in 1995 (*The Economist*, 1997b). And unfortunately, acceleration in the money supply growth rate led to excessive domestic credit creation. Unlike Argentina, however, the resulting deterioration in bank loan quality did not threaten widespread bank insolvencies because of the generally more sound position of the banking system and greater effectiveness of prudential regulations.

What the economic expansion and credit boom did bring about was a surge in imports, which almost doubled from 1992 to 1995. Although merchandise exports grew rapidly too, they did not match the growth in imports, in part because a real appreciation of the rand of approximately 4 percent made South African goods less competitive in international markets. In response to these factors, the South African current account moved from a surplus in 1992 to a deficit that represented about 2.6 percent of GDP in 1995.

The widening current account deficit was sustained by a large capital account surplus. In the 18 months from July 1994 to December 1995, South Africa attracted a net capital inflow. A substantial portion of this inflow, however, was either in the form of short-term lending or portfolio equity investment on the Johannesburg Stock Exchange. In 1995, of the total net inflow of R21.7 billion, 42 percent consisted of short-term capital. Of the long-term capital, that is, capital with an original maturity of greater than one year, more than half consisted of nonresidents' net purchases of securities on the Johannesburg Stock Exchange and on the Bond Exchange of South Africa. These flows, though long-term by definition, in fact are often very volatile.[39]

At the time of the first all-race general election in April 1994, South Africa's net foreign exchange position was near zero (Stals, 1996c). By the end of 1995, the Reserve Bank's net foreign exchange holdings had risen significantly. But the South African balance of payments had also become more sensitive to exchange rate fluctuations. Foreign debt reached $32 billion at the end of 1995 (24 percent of GDP), of which $22.3 billion was foreign-currency denominated. Further, the maturity structure of the debt was becoming increasingly short-term. By 1995, 49 percent of foreign-currency denominated debt fell due within 12 months.

Evolution of the Crisis: The Role of Financial Liberalization

As a result of the build-up in the country's foreign exchange reserves between April 1994 and December 1995, South Africa began to

---

[39] Equity purchases by definition are long-term because there is no maturity date. In practice, however, stock market turnover tends to be quite high.

liberalize its financial markets. In particular, the Reserve Bank relaxed some of its exchange controls. The most important reform was the March 1995 abolishment of the financial rand, a second exchange rate that applied only to nonresident capital account transactions. At the same time, all exchange controls on current account transactions were lifted, including those applied to nonresidents, and South African institutional investors were allowed to hold up to 10 percent of their portfolios in foreign-currency denominated assets. These liberalization measures had profound effects on capital flows, exchange rate fluctuations, the effectiveness and autonomy of monetary policy, and South Africa's vulnerability to external shocks.

Financial liberalization, and the resulting increase in South Africa's integration with world financial markets, influenced the timing and consequent evolution of the rand crisis in at least two ways. First, large and persistent net capital inflows made possible in part by liberalization had caused the rand to appreciate in real terms in 1994 and 1995. Second, a 5-percentage-point rise in interest rates on long-term U.S. Treasury securities in the first few weeks of 1996 lowered investor demand for South African debt instruments. As foreign capital began to flow out as fast as it had flowed in, investors lowered their estimates about the exchange rate the South African economy could support. Unfortunately, the change came suddenly and without much warning.

When the value of the rand first began to fall in mid-February 1996, the Reserve Bank intervened in the foreign exchange markets in order to smooth and control the depreciation process. The result was a nearly 40 percent drop in the level of South Africa's foreign exchange reserves. In addition, the Reserve Bank actively bought the rand on the forward foreign exchange market, increasing its net open position in foreign currency. The central bank intervention, plus a continuous deficit in the overall balance of payments, drained liquidity from the South African banking system and forced up money market interest rates. The political and economic constraints imposed by high unemployment proved too strong to sustain this policy, however, and between January and September 1996 the rand was allowed to depreciate by 22 percent against the U.S. dollar.

The 1996 rand crisis created turmoil in South African financial markets, but it also brought a needed if abrupt adjustment of the overvalued currency. By the end of the year, the South African foreign exchange market had largely stabilized, and the foreign capital position had returned to a net inflow.

Lessons from the South African Currency Crisis

South Africa's currency crisis in 1996 has several interesting features relevant to other EMCs that are trying to manage their integration into world financial markets. First, liberalization of capital controls may encourage capital inflows from short-term foreign investors who find it just as easy to take their money out again in response to domestic and international political and economic developments. Second, an adequate level of foreign exchange reserves is crucial to defending a currency against speculative attack; South Africa was not in a position to protect the rand against a series of determined attacks in early 1996. Third, currency appreciations that result from short-term capital inflows are often not sustainable in the long run, and the external value of the currency may drop dramatically when net capital inflows are suddenly reversed. Fourth, South Africa's currency crisis would likely have been far worse had the South African banking system been less sound. Although unable to prevent the depreciation of the rand, the Reserve Bank was able to keep it from going into a free fall by contracting the monetary base and raising interest rates. This is in sharp contrast to Argentina, where a speculative attack on the peso and resulting rise in interest rates caused losses to the banking system that resulted in widespread insolvency.

Finally, it is interesting that the South African case appears to have had no repercussions for other emerging markets. In contrast to the Mexican peso crisis, which spread to a broad range of EMCs, including South Africa, investors do not appear to have projected South Africa's difficulties onto other EMCs. Explanations may be found by considering in turn each of the indicators of vulnerability to financial contagion described in Table 4.3.

Relevance of Contagion Indicators

Economic linkages. South Africa's economy is largely based on agriculture and mining, and its many competitors in these industries are located throughout the world--from Russia to Brazil to Australia. Few of its competitors have strong economic links to South Africa, which is a true loner country both as a result of its geographical isolation from other developed capital markets and because of its past status as an international political pariah. The economic-linkages model suggests, therefore, that the rapid depreciation of the rand did not spread to other countries because the negative effects on other economies were limited.

Heightened awareness. Another possible explanation for the lack of contagion is that South Africa's recent rehabilitation in the international political sphere makes it a special case in the minds of investors. Therefore, even if South Africa's fundamentals were similar to those of other countries, they may have believed that its experience would not be transferable.

Portfolio adjustment. Because of South Africa's geographical isolation from other EMCs, it is not consistently grouped with other countries in regional portfolios. Capital flight from South Africa, therefore, would be unlikely to spark liquidity-related redemptions of other countries' assets in any meaningful way.

Herd behavior. Although the capital inflows that South Africa received between April 1994 and December 1995 were large relative to previous years, they were not large relative to investment flows in other parts of the world. For example, the average value of South African international equity issues between 1992 and 1995 was just U.S. $184 million, as compared to $2,282 million for Mexico and $474 million for Thailand. Similarly, there were just 17 Africa-oriented mutual funds with net assets of $600 million in 1995. In comparison, in 1995 there were 147 Latin American regional mutual funds with net assets of $8.5 billion, and 305 Asian regional mutual funds with net assets of

$34.8 billion.[40] South Africa was clearly not a popular investment destination for large numbers of possibly impressionable retail investors.

Case Study 3: Thailand

In contrast to the Argentine and South African cases, the Thai financial crisis that resulted in a forced depreciation of the baht in July 1997 had been simmering for well over a year. A three-year property slump and the slowest economic growth in a decade put severe pressure on the Thai banking system, which like so many EMC banking systems is plagued by "insider" lending and poor loan quality. Worries about the economy and the overvalued baht contributed to a 60 percent decline in the benchmark Stock Exchange of Thailand (SET) stock index between February 1996 and May 1997, and a further 20 percent decline between May and August 1997. The baht itself had been under intermittently severe pressure for several months before its ultimate collapse.

In September 1996, Moody's Investors Services downgraded Thailand's short-term debt rating, citing the country's overreliance on short-term debt to finance persistent current-account deficits. In December, the central bank spent about 2.3 percent of its foreign exchange reserves in defense of the baht, which had been the subject of devaluation rumors. On February 14, 1997, another speculative attack temporarily dropped the value of the baht by almost 1 percent against the dollar, and the benchmark SET index fell by 4.5 percent. Both moves were in response to a suggestion that Thailand's sovereign credit rating might be cut. In March, a run on bank deposits led to an estimated withdrawal of more than $1.2 billion from 91 finance companies. On April 10, Moody's Investors Services did downgrade Thailand's long-term sovereign credit rating, as well as the bond and deposit rating for five Thai banks. Finally, despite statements by the Thai government that it would "fight

---

[40] Some Asian regional funds include Japan (IMF, 1996).

to the death" to defend the baht, the Bank of Thailand eliminated the baht's official trading band on July 2 and moved to a managed float.

Evolution of the Thai Crisis: A Classic Crisis Scenario

In many ways, the Thai case represents the classic case of an EMC financial crisis. Until fairly recently, Thailand was one of the fastest growing emerging markets. From the late 1980s to the mid-1990s, Thai GDP grew at an average rate of 8.5 percent. Equity and real estate markets boomed as exports soared and Thai banks and finance companies raced to distribute approximately 400 billion baht in housing and commercial development loans (Pura, 1997). Often there was little careful assessment of the creditworthiness of borrowers, and lenders also neglected to consider potential market volatility and cash flow analysis in their quest for growth. In fact, Thai financial institutions paid more attention to the valuation of collateral, such as property and stocks, than to the reputation of their borrowers.

As in South Africa, deregulation and liberalization of Thailand's financial sector also played a role in the financial crisis. In the early 1990s, Thailand relaxed its foreign exchange controls in order to allow easy access to foreign capital markets. As a result, major banks and financial companies soon became burdened by foreign debt. Liberalization also had another downside. It increased competition among lenders and cut profitable interest margins between lending and borrowing. Because other financial institutions such as leasing firms and credit-card companies also had access to foreign capital markets, banks and finance companies were forced to accept more risks and lend aggressively in order to maintain market share.

Foreign capital inflows contributed to the credit boom and consequent overvaluation of Thai financial assets. Low interest rates and recession in the United States and other developed markets in the late 1980s and early 1990s made Thailand, as well as other emerging markets, attractive to foreign portfolio investors. In addition, Thai banks and financial institutions took advantage of low foreign interest rates to borrow dollars abroad and re-lend them to domestic customers at much higher rates in baht. Because the baht was effectively pegged to the dollar, foreign exchange risks were perceived to be minimal and profits seemed guaranteed. Much of the foreign borrowing was short-term, but it was used to finance long-term loans in baht. This created a mismatch in terms of both maturity and currency on bank balance sheets.

But in 1995-1996 the U.S. dollar appreciated sharply against the Japanese yen. Due to the effective dollar peg, the baht also appreciated against the yen in real terms. The rising yen/baht exchange rate raised the yen cost of Thai products and undermined their competitiveness in important Japanese markets. Exports fell. By the third quarter of 1996, the Thai current account deficit equaled $16 billion or 8 percent of GDP, approximately the same size as Mexico's before the peso collapse in December 1994 (*The Economist*, 1997a). By February 1997, it had increased to $22.5 billion (*The Asian Wall Street Journal*, 1997). Real economic growth, which in 1995 averaged 8.6 percent, fell to 6.4 percent in 1996; prior to the baht devaluation, official forecasts for 1997 put the growth rate below 5 percent (Vatikiotis, 1997).

When the bubble burst, the value of bank and finance company assets fell quickly. Interest rate increases designed to defend the baht also heightened bankruptcy rates among property developers and financial companies and worsened the banks' predicament. Foreign creditors started to pull back as doubt over the asset quality of Thai banks and financial institutions grew. In the first two months of 1997, the interbank overnight rate rose from 10 percent to 12 percent (Pura, 1997). Thailand's apparent political inability to deal with the crisis, further revelations of high-level corruption, and the June resignation of a respected finance minister did little to restore investors' confidence. Like Argentina, a major balance-of-payments crisis eventually forced Thailand to submit to an IMF-administered rescue plan involving a credit line of up to $15 billion (Tasker, 1997).

Lessons from the Thai Financial Crisis: An Asian Mexico?

Even before the forced devaluation of the baht, Thailand's financial troubles had begun to spread to other countries in the region.

For example, on May 15, 1997, the Indonesian rupiah and Malaysian ringgit both fell sharply in response to a May 14 attack that had briefly forced the baht below its official trading band. Share prices on East Asian equity markets also fell: by 2.9 percent in Kuala Lumpur, 2.4 percent in Manila, and 2 percent in Jakarta.

But the greatest turbulence has come since Thailand devalued the baht on July 2. The Philippine peso was effectively devalued on July 11, falling 9.8 percent in a single day. On July 23-24, the ringgit, rupiah, and Singapore dollar, as well as the baht, once again came under severe speculative pressure, and there were unsuccessful attacks on the Korean won and the Hong Kong dollar. On August 14, Indonesia floated the rupiah. Malaysia, which has come under periodic severe attacks, has experimented with several different types of capital controls in order to contain "immoral" currency traders. Stock markets around the region have suffered dramatic losses.

There were some traditional indicators of vulnerability to financial crisis in Asia. Most of the East Asian economies had started to slow down in 1996 and were predicted to slow further.[41] Nevertheless, these estimates still represent robust economic growth. Overlending was also a problem for banking systems throughout East Asia as well as Thailand. But the problem was recognized if not adequately addressed by policymakers. In Singapore, steps were taken in May 1996 to cool down property markets, although by April 1997 property loans still accounted for about 33 percent of banks' total loans. Malaysia and the Philippines also imposed measures to control the growth of property loans in early 1997.[42]

---

[41] Goldman-Sachs (Asia), as quoted in Webb (1997b), estimated that real GDP growth rate in Indonesia would fall from a peak of 8.2 percent in 1995 to under 7.2 percent in 1997, Malaysia would slow from 9.5 percent in 1996 to 7.5 percent in 1997, and Singapore would fall from 8.8 percent to 6.5 percent in 1997.

[42] Government officials in Singapore redefined capital gains on real estate as income for tax purposes and imposed a 3 percent "stamp duty" on new properties and properties sold within three years of being purchased (Chang *et al*, 1997). In the Malaysia, the central bank imposed a 20 percent limit on banks' exposure to the property sector (Yee, 1997). A similar action was taken by the Philippine central bank one month later (Webb and Reyes, 1997).

In addition, all of the East Asian countries received substantial capital inflows during the 1990s, and East Asian banking systems were not slow to borrow from international capital markets in order to extend credit domestically. In the Philippines, for example, foreign currency-denominated bank loans grew 284 percent from 1994 to 1997 (Webb, 1997a). There were few dramatic changes to justify the panic of investors on purely country-specific grounds, however, unfortunately for the Southeast Asian EMCs, their vulnerability to externally generated contagion was high.

Relevance of Contagion Indicators

Economic linkages. Industries such as semiconductors and textiles are highly concentrated in the region, with the Southeast Asian EMCs seeing each other as their greatest competitors. Investors may have legitimately worried that, in the face of a baht devaluation, firms based in Indonesia, Malaysia, and the Philippines might no longer be competitive with firms based in Thailand. Financial connections within the region are also strong; for example, Singapore-based banks had extensive foreign-currency lending commitments in Thailand and Malaysia, so that the baht devaluation had an immediate impact on their balance sheets.

Heightened awareness. As discussed above, Thailand's real estate and banking troubles reverberated with investors in other East Asian EMCs. In particular, investors may have worried that there were other financial skeletons, such as imminent banking-sector scandals and collapses, lurking in the neighbors' closets. Also, investors may have worried that regional institutional arrangements, such as swap agreements and liquidity arrangements, would not go through in the face of a generalized attack on several regional currencies at once.

Portfolio adjustment. As in the case of Argentina and Latin America, individual East Asian countries are heavily grouped in Asian regional portfolios by investors. Although direct investment has traditionally formed a much higher proportion of capital inflows in Malaysia (for example) than in Thailand, a stable exchange rate environment had encouraged the growth of fixed-income mutual funds throughout the region.

Herd behavior. East Asia was the darling of international investors throughout the early 1990s, many of whom were small-scale retail investors. Such sudden, huge, short-term capital inflows are highly vulnerable to changes in investor sentiment, which were probably triggered by events in Thailand.

6. CONCLUSION

Why do some crises appear to be contagious? And why do some emerging financial markets appear to be vulnerable to contagion while others do not? These questions are important because apparently contagious asset price collapses threaten ongoing efforts to increase the efficiency of world markets through financial market deregulation. Governments, particularly in EMCs, may place restrictions on cross-border capital flows in response to what they claim to be irrational and capricious investor behavior over which they have no control. Perhaps more important, contagious crises directly threaten the economic interests of the United States and other developed nations with whom the EMCs have significant trade and investment ties. The expansion of a crisis increases the likelihood that the countries affected will require international assistance to regain the confidence of investors and recover economic and financial stability.

Defining a crisis as a very large decline in either the U.S. dollar value of the local currency or a broad-based stock price index, we propose three reasons why countries might experience crises at the same, or close to the same, time: coincidence, a common external shock to economic conditions across countries, and a contagious loss of confidence in local financial markets as a result of an external financial crisis. We argue that, to the extent that crises are coincidental--that is, country-specific in origin--in many, if not most cases, they should be both predictable and preventable with the help of traditional economic warning signals. To the extent that crises are externally generated, however, traditional warning signals may be of little use.

We begin with an analysis of weekly stock price and currency-exchange-rate data for 23 countries, six of which are considered to have developed financial markets and 17 of which are still emerging. Our crisis identification methodology suggests that contemporaneous financial collapses involving multiple countries were not uncommon. Between January 1989 and August 1997, we identify eleven separate episodes in which four or more countries were involved. Of these, the majority reflected primarily stock market, as opposed to currency market, turbulence. An examination of English-language press accounts and other publications, however, indicates that the majority of these multicountry crises were not contagious. Most originated in the countries where they occurred. Inappropriate macroeconomic policies, domestic political struggles, and, as a distant third, sheer bad luck were identified as the major factors contributing to severe asset market turbulence. In these cases, governments would not be justified in blaming external events for domestic asset price collapses.

However, five of our eleven episodes do appear to have been at least partly driven by either a common external shock or financial contagion. Episode 2 (following the Tiananmen Square massacre in China), which saw stock markets throughout East Asia sliding steeply, is identified as a common-shock episode. Episode 3, which followed the October 13, 1989, crash of the U.S. market, suggests that loss of confidence in the U.S. stock market was contagious, spreading to Germany, Singapore, and the United Kingdom, and possibly to Malaysia and Turkey as well. The Iraqi invasion of Kuwait, which inaugurated episode 5, had a common impact on many countries; in all, twelve countries experienced stock market collapses during the week ending August 24, 1990. Finally, the collapses of the Mexican peso in December 1994 and the Thai baht in July 1997 both appear to have had unfortunate consequences for countries well beyond their borders. In the months surrounding these last two episodes, tests of statistical causality suggest that stock and currency market collapses in numerous countries were driven by events in Mexico and Thailand.

These externally generated crisis episodes may have been outside the power of individual governments to prevent. This does not mean, however, that the way in which the crises spread was impossible to predict. The three contagious crisis episodes, and particularly the two later episodes involving mostly EMC markets, might well have been predicted by the proper set of indicators. We believe that models of the crisis transmission mechanism could potentially provide far better crisis warning signals than more traditional indicators of economic and financial vulnerability. Given a country experiencing financial troubles, these models could help to tell us whether other markets are vulnerable to contagion and, if so, which ones.

We do not attempt, in this paper, to formalize the four models of the crisis transmission mechanism that we develop. Instead, we conduct three informal case studies of EMCs in crisis to determine whether our contagion crisis indicators might have had predictive power. The first case, Argentina after the devaluation of the Mexican peso in December 1994, suggests that the economic-linkages model did not apply. The other three models of financial contagion, however, appear to be relevant: the crisis in Mexico may have focused attention on existing financial problems in Argentina, Argentina probably suffered from the disadvantage of being grouped with Mexico in regional investment portfolios, and Argentina had attracted many retail investors who may have dumped Argentine assets at the first sign of trouble in Latin America.

In contrast, South Africa's currency crisis of 1996 provides an example of the "dog that didn't bark." With no strong economic or financial ties to other countries, a unique recent economic and political history, no involvement in regional investment portfolios, and limited attraction for retail investors, South Africa's crisis passed almost unnoticed by investors and other EMCs.

Finally, the financial turbulence experienced by Southeast Asian EMCs--and now East Asia in general--after the devaluation of the Thai baht in July 1997 has had an impact on the United States and other financial centers, and is likely to have a lasting impact on the countries of the region. This case provides perhaps the clearest example of the failure of traditional indicators. As we show, the Indonesian, Malaysian, and Philippine economies were not demonstrably weaker just prior to the crisis than they had been two years previously, but their vulnerability to contagion from Thailand was nevertheless strong. All four of the crisis transmission mechanisms were relevant: strong economic linkages within the region, similar problems related to banking and real estate, common membership in regional investment portfolios, and the potential to become "fallen angels," deserted as quickly as they were embraced by a fickle investor community.

BIBLIOGRAPHY

The Asian Wall Street Journal, "Thai Current-Account Trade Deficits Widen," March 31, 1997, p. 5.

Baillie, Richard, and Timothy Bollerslev, "The Message in Daily Exchange Rates: A Conditional-Variance Tale," *Journal of Business and Economic Statistics*, Vol. 7, 1989, pp. 297-305.

Banerjee, Abhijit V., "A Simple Model of Herd Behavior," *Quarterly Journal of Economics*, Vol. 107, No. 3, August 1992, pp. 797-817.

Calvo, Guillermo A., and Enrique G. Mendoza, "Mexico's Balance of Payments Crisis: A Chronicle of a Death Foretold," *Journal of International Economics*, Vol. 41, November 1996, pp. 235-64.

Calvo, Sara, and Carmen M. Reinhart, "Capital Flows to Latin America: Is There Evidence of Contagion Effects," paper prepared for a conference on *Private Capital Flows to Emerging Markets*, Vienna, September 7-9, 1995.

Caprio, Gerard Jr., and Daniela Klingebiel, "Bank Insolvencies: Cross-Country Experience," World Bank Policy Research Working Paper No. 1620, Washington, D.C.: World Bank, July 1996.

Chang, Yin-Hsin, Sara Webb, G. Pierre Goad, Darren McDermott, Rexie Reyes, and Raphael Pura, "Officials in Asia Try to Head Off Property Woes," *The Asian Wall Street Journal*, April 7, 1997, p. 1.

Chuhan, Punam, Gabriel Perez-Quiros, and Helen Popper, "The Capital Flow Mix: Foreign Direct Investment, Short-Term Investment, and Other Ingredients," Unpublished working paper, August 1997.

The Economist, "Mahathir's Roasting," September 27, 1997a, p. 39.

The Economist, "Thailand: Taking a Baht," February 22, 1997b, pp. 84-85.

The Economist, "South Africa's Economy: Turnaround," March 8, 1997c, pp. 89-90.

Eichengreen, Barry, Andrew K. Rose, and Charles Wyplosz, "Exchange Market Mayhem: The Antecedents and Aftermath of Speculative Attacks," *Economic Policy*, 1995.

Frankel, Jeffrey A., and Andrew K. Rose, "Currency Crashes in Emerging Markets: An Empirical Treatment," *Journal of International Economics*, Vol. 41, November 1996, pp. 351-368.

Frankel, Jeffrey A., and Sergio Schmukler, "Crisis, Contagion, and Country Funds: Effects on East Asia and Latin America," Center for

Pacific Basin Monetary and Economic Studies Working Paper PB96-04, Federal Reserve Bank of San Francisco, September 1996.

Garber, Peter, and Subir Lall, "Derivative Products in Exchange Rate Crises," Paper prepared for the Federal Reserve Bank of San Francisco's conference on Managing Capital Flows and Exchange Rates: Lessons from the Pacific Basin," San Francisco, CA, September 26-27, 1996.

Gerlach, Stefan, and Frank Smets, "Contagious Speculative Attacks," Bank for International Settlements Working Paper, September 1994.

Geweke, John, Richard Meese, and William Dent, "Comparing Alternative Tests of Causality in Temporal Systems," *Journal of Econometrics*, Vol. 21, 1982, pp. 161-194.

Huh, Chan, and Kenneth Kasa, "A Dynamic Model of Export Competition, Policy Coordination, and Simultaneous Currency Collapse," Center for Pacific Basin Monetary and Economic Studies Working Paper PB97-08, Federal Reserve Bank of San Francisco, September 1997.

International Finance Corporation (IFC), *Emerging Stock Markets Factbook*, Washington, D.C.: IFC, various years.

International Monetary Fund (IMF), *International Capital Markets: Systemic Issues in International Finance*, IMF World Economic and Financial Surveys, Washington, D.C.: IMF, August 1993.

International Monetary Fund (IMF), *International Capital Markets: Developments, Prospects, and Policy Issues*, IMF World Economic and Financial Surveys, Washington, D.C.: IMF, August 1995.

International Monetary Fund (IMF), *International Capital Markets: Developments, Prospects, and Key Policy Issues*, IMF World Economic and Financial Surveys, Washington, D.C.: IMF, September 1996.

International Monetary Fund (IMF), *International Financial Statistics*, Washington, D.C.: IMF, various issues.

Kaminsky, Graciela, Saul Lizondo, and Carmen M. Reinhart, "Leading Indicators of Currency Crises," Working Paper of the International Monetary Fund, No. WP/97/79, July 1997.

Kaminsky, Graciela, and Carmen M. Reinhart, "The Twin Crises: The Causes of Banking and Balance of Payments Problems," Unpublished working paper, September 1996.

Lindgren, Carl-Johan, Gillian Garcia, and Matthew I. Saal, *Bank Soundness and Macroeconomic Policy*, Washington, D.C.: IMF, 1996.

Meese, Richard A., and Andrew K. Rose, "Exchange Rate Instability: Determinants and Predictability," Unpublished working paper, Haas School of Business, University of California, Berkeley, August 1996.

Ministry of Economy and Public Works, Republic of Argentina, *Economic Report: First Quarter 1995,* No. 13 (on-line publication available at http://www.mecon.ar).

Mishkin, Frederic S., "Asymmetric Information and Financial Crises: A Historical Perspective," in R. Glenn Hubbard, ed., *Financial Markets and Financial Crises*, Chicago: The University of Chicago Press, 1991.

Nelson, Daniel, "Conditional Heteroskedasticity in Asset Returns: A New Approach," *Econometrica*, Vol. 59, 1991, pp. 347–370.

Popper, Helen, and Julia Lowell, "Officially Floating, Implicitly Targeted Exchange Rates: Examples from the Pacific Basin," in Michael Hutchison and Reuven Glick, eds., *Exchange Rate Policy and Interdependence: Perspectives from the Pacific Basin*, Cambridge: Cambridge University Press, 1994.

Pura, Raphael, "How Optimism Built—And Doomed—A Thai Empire," *The Asian Wall Street Journal*, March 31, 1997, p. 1.

Sachs, Jeffrey D., Aaron Tornell, and Andres Velasco, "Financial Crises in Emerging Markets: The Lessons from 1995," *Brookings Papers on Economic Activity*, Volume 1, 1996.

Scharfstein, David S., and Jeremy C. Stein, "Herd Behavior and Investment," *American Economic Review*, Vol. 80, 1990, pp. 465-79.

South African Reserve Bank, *Annual Report 1996* (on-line publication available at http://www.resbank.co.za).

Stals, Chris, "The Integration of South Africa in the World Financial Markets," Address by the Governor of the South African Reserve Bank, Durban, March 7, 1996a (available on-line at http://resbank.co.za).

Stals, Chris, "Monetary Policy and Inflation Targets," Address by the Governor of the South African Reserve Bank at the Annual General Meeting of the South Africa/Canada Chamber of Commerce, Johannesburg, May 2, 1996b (available on-line at http://resbank.co.za).

Stals, Chris, "South Africa: What to Expect?" Address by the Governor of the South African Reserve Bank at the Massachusetts Institute of Technology, Cambridge, MA, October 2, 1996c (available on-line at http://resbank.co.za).

Tasker, Rodney, "The First Step: Thailand Agrees to an IMF Rescue Plan," *Far Eastern Economic Review,* August 14, 1997, p. 52.

Vatikiotis, Michael, "Off the Peg, On the Rack," *Far Eastern Economic Review,* July 17, 1997, pp. 74-76.

Webb, Sara, "After Thailand, Where Next for Disaster?" *The Asian Wall Street Journal*, April 23, 1997a, p. 1.

Webb, Sara, "Asian Banks Pose New Challenges for Investors," *The Asian Wall Street Journal*, May 8, 1997b, p. 13.

Webb, Sara, and Rexie Reyes, "Philippines Puts Cap on Property Lending," *The Asian Wall Street Journal*, April 30, 1997, p. 1.

Wolf, Holger C., "Co-Movements Among Emerging Equity Markets," Paper prepared for the Federal Reserve Bank of San Francisco's conference on Managing Capital Flows and Exchange Rates: Lessons from the Pacific Basin, San Francisco, September 26-27, 1996.

Yee, Chen May, "Malaysia Signals Caution with Curbs on Lending," *The Asian Wall Street Journal*, March 31, 1997, p. 1.